Joshua Thomas, David Jones

A History of the Baptist Association in Wales

from the year 1650, to the year 1790

Joshua Thomas, David Jones

A History of the Baptist Association in Wales
from the year 1650, to the year 1790

ISBN/EAN: 9783337328795

Printed in Europe, USA, Canada, Australia, Japan

Cover: Foto ©Lupo / pixelio.de

More available books at **www.hansebooks.com**

A

HISTORY

OF THE

BAPTIST ASSOCIATION

IN

WALES,

FROM THE YEAR 1650, TO THE YEAR 1790,

SHEWING

THE TIMES AND PLACES OF THEIR ANNUAL MEETINGS,

WHETHER

IN WALES, LONDON, OR BRISTOL, &c.

INCLUDING

SEVERAL OTHER INTERESTING ARTICLES.

BY JOSHUA THOMAS

OF LEOMINSTER.

LONDON:

Sold by Messrs. Dilly, Button, and Thomas, London; Brown, James, and Cottle, Bristol; Ogle, Edinburgh; Allein, Dublin; and may be had of the *Baptist Ministers* in New York, Philadelphia, Boston, Richmond, Savannah, and Charleston, in America.

1795.

This History was printed in the Baptist Register, only a sheet at a time occasionally, as the Editor of that work found room. This accounts for the appearance of the first sheet of it in 1791, and for the publication of the last, not till 1795—the date which is in the title page. Several Ministers who were alive when the first sheet came out died before the last was printed.

AN ADDRESS TO THE READER.

THE History of the Baptist churches in Wales was published in Welsh in 1778. There was a motion made to the Author to undertake it near 30 years before. He then had very little idea of it. Not long after, it occasionally engaged his attention. About 1752, he began to pick up a few hints, as they fell in his way. In 1754, he removed to Leominster, in Herefordshire. Thus leaving the Principality he almost gave up every thought of the subject; but judged it proper to put the few fragments he had obtained into some order, and then send them into Wales to be circulated and improved in the best manner they could. He did so. One looked over them and said, he could add nothing: another did the same. The Author being at the Association in Wales, in 1770, was reminded of the History. He related what he had done, and was urged to resume the work. He made a kind of a promise to do so if no body else would undertake it.

About that time Mr. Thompson of London was collecting a brief account of the Dissenters of the three denominations through England and Wales. A letter was sent to the Author at Leominster on the subject, which induced him to set about this long suspended article. His mind bent to it with a degree of resolution, he thought—he recollected---wrote letters, and in short, did all that his confined situation, preaching four or five times a week, and teaching a school, would admit. In 1776, he took a short tour through South Wales. He made the Association in his round; was from home about six weeks, and collected materials. On his return, perusing his papers, deficiencies soon appeared. He wrote to one place and another for additions and explanations, closely pursuing the business. In the spring 1777, a few advertisements were printed off, and circulated among the churches, informing them of the state of the work, and desiring them to consult among themselves whether it should be prosecuted or dropped; and to give him their opinion at the Association. Accordingly he found that every church wished to have the History printed. The number agreed to be taken amounted to about 800, and 1s. a book subscription money was paid, and 1200 were printed.

In a short Epistle to the Reader, the Author observed, that as the work was the first essay upon an obscure subject, no body could well expect it to be perfect; but that if any mistakes were discovered he would gratefully receive information. When the Book was circulated, remarks were made, some right, and some wrong;

wrong; some in a friendly way, others not quite so; but the Writer availed himself all he could of every information, not regarding whether it came from a friend or a foe. In about twenty months 18 pages of *Addenda* and *Corrigenda* were printed off, of the same size as the book, and circulated gratis, that those who chose it might bind them with the book. Thus far the Writer did what he could.

In 1781, Mr. Backus's Church History of New England, fell into his hands. There he found an account of Ilston church, near Swansea, of which he had no hint before, but what appeared in an old book of church records in Abergavenny. By the New England History, it appeared, that a neat church-book had been carried from Ilston to America, containing a particular account of the Baptist churches in Wales, about the year 1650, and that the book was still in being. It is easy to conceive, that the Author of the Welsh History much wished to see that book. But the American war, and a number of other hindrances, seemed to render it impossible. He wrote to Mr. Backus in 1783. He very soon, and very obligingly answered, and wrote large Extracts out of it, of what he judged most to the purpose. These cast considerable light upon what was before impenetrably dark. In Page 5, of the History, those Extracts are referred to. They came in 1784; and now it was strongly concluded, that, on this subject, there was still more light to be derived from the Ilston book, than could be had any where else upon earth. Impelled by hope, several queries more were framed, and a second application made in 1785. But for three years no answer came. The Author had mentioned in the Welsh History, his design to draw up a short account of the Welsh Association, if life and health continued. He was not willing to set about it till the second Extracts arrived. In 1788, he wrote again. Age coming on, a Baptist Register being likely to appear, and other things conspiring, the Writer set about *the History of the Association*, without the advantage of the second Extracts. He finished it and sent the Manuscript to London for the Register. But still lamented the disappointment of further intelligence, which he was confident might be had in the book. One sheet was printed in the second Number of that work, Aug. 1791. This happened to be the very part which chiefly wanted the additional information. In that year Dr. Rippon writing to Mr. Backus obligingly mentioned the disappointment. Mr. Backus was struck, and replied, that the letters of 1785 and 1788 had duly come to hand, and that he had sent large Extracts, and a long letter in 1787; but says, he never could learn whether they were received or not, till Brother Rippon's letter came in October 1791. He took the first opportunity and made large extracts containing sixty-four quarto pages: and his letter says, " I got the book, and now send you *all* the light I can get from thence, about the history of your country." Yet before it came, a second sheet of the History of the Association was printed off, in the Regifter, fo that it was impoffible to rectify miftakes but by fome fuch addrefs as this. And thefe are the chief reafons for it.

There were two circumftances that occafioned fome miftakes, which muft have remained for ever, in all probability, had not the fecond Extracts arrived to rectify them. One happened thus. About 1752, the Writer found fome old loofe papers at Abergavenny, out of which he tranfcribed what appeared to his purpofe. But there happened a miftake of a fingle letter either in the original Writer, or the Tranfcriber. The proper word was *Llanaran*, and it was tranfcribed *Llanavan*. The Writer well knew a place of the latter name near Builth, in Brecknockfhire, and that there were Baptifts there about the year 1650, but had not the leaft idea of a place of the former name in the whole world; fo the laft was taken to be right without any hefitation, and it was printed thus thro' the Welfh Hiftory and thro' moft of the Englifh Hiftory of the Affociation. But what was faid of the Baptifts in Llanavan remains true, yet there are fome little miftakes in connexions. The fecond Extracts fhew plainly, that there was a place called *Llanaran*, there written *Llanharan*. Hence the Author wrote to a friend in Monmouthfhire, defiring him to enquire whether there be a place of the name in that county, or in Glamorganfhire. He was informed, that *Llanharan*, or properly *Llanaran*, is about three miles from the town of Llantrifaint, in the county of Glamorgan. Thus the difficulty was quite cleared up.

The fecond miftake was about the town of *Llantrifaint*, juft now mentioned. There is a parifh of the fame name in Monmouthfhire. The Writer knew very well that there had been Baptifts that way ever fince 1640, but never had heard of any in the former place. Yet the fecond Extracts evidently prove, that the fame church which was formed at *Llanaran* in 1650, met foon after in the town of *Llantrifaint*. But before that information came, the place in Glamorganfhire was taken for that in Monmouthfhire. All this is no great injury to the real Hiftory, as what is faid of the Baptifts in Monmouthfhire ftill remains true. Yet, as better light came, and as it pleafed God to continue life and health, the Writer thinks it a duty he owes the public and himfelf to give the reafons of the miftakes, and to confefs and rectify them with his own hand. He likewife has written out, in *Englifh*, the hiftory of the churches concerned, and affected in the firft and fecond Extracts, and tranfcribed the fubftance of the two Extracts, in their proper places. That hiftory may not be printed in the Author's life time, yet he is glad that the Extracts are diftributed to the beft advantage he was capable of, that Mr. Backus's labour of love may not be in vain.

EXPLANATIONS AND ADDITIONS,

(WITH ERRORS OF THE PRESS RECTIFIED,)

Made from *Second Extracts* sent by the Rev. Mr. Backus of Middleborough, after part of this History was printed.

Page 4, line 7, &c. from the bottom, *for* " a petition was sent to the King shewing, humbly and truly, by many respectable persons to the King and Parliament," *read,* " it was humbly and truly presented in a petition, by many respectable persons, to the King and Parliament."

P, 5, *l.* 17. *for* Mr. P. *r.* Mr. Powell.

P. 6, *l.* 4. *dele* very probably.

Ibid. *l.* 7. *after* 1650, *r.* or rather about the middle of the 12th month, 1649.

——— *l.* 11, *for* Llanafan, *r.* Llanaran, and *dele* pronounced Llanavan.

——— *l.* 13, 31, *for* Llanafan, *r.* Llanaran.

P. 6. *after l.* 11, *r.* thus, out of Mr. Backus's extracts, " These three churches being thus settled, the Lord's goodness is still extended to us, insomuch that they are very much increased, both with gifts and members to the praise of his great name: and being thus settled through grace, they bethought themselves how to carry on the work in Wales; and therefore mutually agreed, that upon the 6th and 7th days of the 9th month, they would have a general meeting at Ilston, of the members of each church. So accordingly it was performed." This paragraph will explain page 7, three first lines. Add further, " A church was constituted at Carmarthen on the 22d of the 11th month 1650." The second extracts give no exact date when any church was formed but this: yet it is plain enough, that Ilston, Hay, and Llanaran were formed before Carmarthen.

P. 7, *l.* 17, *for* Llanafan, *r.* Llanaran.

Ibid. *l.* 22, *for* three Months, *r.* four Months.

——— *l.* 40, *add,* the second Extracts mention, that at a meeting on the 16th of the 5th month, 1651, reference was had to a general meeting at Llanaran as then past. But the Extracts contain no full account of any other general meetings, though they give hints of a few. It does not appear that the minutes in 1650 and 1651 were signed by the Association.

P. 8, *l.* 14, *for* Monmouthshire, *r.* Glamorganshire. And there *dele* " and was," with the two lines 15, 16. Then add, " It seems they found a more convenient place at Llantrisaint than at Llanaran, as the latter occurs no more."

P. 8, all, from line 16 to the bottom, but the two last lines, is the effect of the mistake about Llanafan. But the narrative there is true, understood of Llanafan in Brecknockshire. Now it appears plain enough by the second Extracts, that Llanafan was not in connexion with the Association in the time of the Commonwealth; nor is there any hint of that church in the narratives of the London Assemblies of 1689, &c.

And to the Note in that page, *add,* There are two more of the family in the ministry, Mr. John Evans, a General Baptist in London, and Mr. James Jarman, a Conformist in the Establishment.

P. 15, *l.* 25, by the second Extracts, and the letter sent with them, it does not appear that any account is recorded in Ilston book of the Hay Meeting, nor much inserted of any thing after 1653, except some letters, and their own church affairs. Not a word, it seems, of the General Meeting at Aberafon, a branch of their own church, nor of the meetings at Llantrisaint and Brecknock.

P. 17,

EXPLANATIONS AND ADDITIONS. vii

P. 17, &c. Names several ministers in Wales. The following, unless one or two who died before the Restoration, are supposed to have finished their course during the persecutions from 1660 to 1688. Messrs. Vavasor Powell, Jenkin Jones, Henry Williams, John Myles, Hugh Evans, Anthony Harry, Morgan Jones, Morgan Jones, Thomas Proud, Thomas Joseph, Thomas Jones, Howel Thomas, Walter Proffer, William Thomas, David Davis, Howel Vaughan. Several more are mentioned in the second Extracts, as very useful helps; particularly Evan Llewelyn and David Thomas. Evan Bowen of Llanafan also was a noted minister. Dr. Walker says he had 4000 souls under his care: his large parish is meant. The following worthies survived the grievous persecutions; Messrs. Christopher Price, Thomas Watkins, William Prichard, Lewis Thomas, Robert Morgan, Griffith Howells, William Jones, Thomas Quarrell, Thomas Evans, Henry Gregory, Francis Giles, Thomas David Rees, Thomas Parry, John Edwards, William Milman; Robert Morgan, &c. It is probable that most of these had begun to preach before 1660, but they lived till the year 1688, and several of them long after. A considerable number of excellent men entered upon the ministry before the persecution ended at the Revolution, as Messrs. James James, George Jones, Samuel Jones, John Jenkins, Nathaniel Morgan, Evan David, Richard Williams, Joseph Price, &c. Here are above forty ministers of the Baptist denomination in the Principality before 1688, most of them men of worth and note in their day.

P. 18, l. 35, By the second extracts, we learn that Lewis Thomas was baptized in 1650, and was a stated minister in 1657.

P. 20, l. 17, *dele* all of it after Kelligar, and all line 18 wholly.

Ibid. l. 30, *add* Thomas Evans.

P. 21, l. 31, Francis Giles is put wrong in the printed narrative of the London Assembly of 1689. He should have been inserted there for Llanwenarth, and Robert Morgan for Swansea. The latter then complained of that error in a letter to London, which was seen by the Writer of this history. Thus there were seven messengers from Wales at the London Assembly that year.

Ibid l. 35, *for* thirty-eight, r. thirty-seven.

P. 22, l. 9, *after* met, put a semicolon. Llantrisaint is the name of the place in Monmouthshire. The church there at that time met in three different places, Llangwm, Llantrisaint, and Abergavenny.

P. 23, l. 18, *for* church r. churches.

Ibid. l. 35, &c. The arrangement of the churches here is not quite accurate, it would be better thus; Ilston, then called Swansea; Hay, resuming the old name Olchon; Craig-yr-allt instead of Llantrisaint, and Llanaran, Glamorganshire; Llanwenarth instead of the former Abergavenny; Carmarthen broke up, and the remaining members joined to the Carmarthenshire part of Swansea church; Llanfaches in Monmouthshire, was formed in 1639, but was a mixture of Baptists and Independents, therefore not in the association of 1651, &c. But sometime after the Baptist part formed a society by themselves, and met to worship in the three places above named. The names of the churches in 1690 stood thus; Swansea, Olchon, Craig-yr-allt, Llanwenarth, and Llangwm, five, as in 1655: but the names all changed. Carmarthen was dissolved, and Llangwm brought in; the church west of Carmarthen met in three places, that made the number six. But Blaenau was a branch of Llanwenarth, yet so distant that it was called a church, though not then properly incorporated. They sent a separate letter to London in 1690. And in a letter of that year, sent by Mr. Robert Morgan to London, he says, they were then seven churches in the connexion, which are to be understood in the above order, not yet reckoning Llanafan and Radnor.

Ibid. l. 43, *for* 168-, r. 1689, and l. 46, for M. r. Mr.

N. B. The paragraph at the foot of page 23, and at the top of p. 24, is true in fact, with this exception, that the church never had been in the Association, so had never left it. Probably it was also then a
mix

mixt fociety, and had been long fo. The feventh church was numbered as above, and omitting Radnor as in that paragraph.

P. 24, *l.* 32, The narrative of the London Affembly, of 1689, mentions only fix, but there fhould have been feven minifters inferted from Wales, as already noted, and five in 1691.

P. 25, *l.* 22, *for* many, *r.* feveral.

P. 29, *l.* 9, *underftand* Llantrifaint here in connexion with Llangwm, and fo in any following place where Llantrifaint may occur. In this page, and the preceding, we have the firft proper account of Llanafan and Radnor joining the connexion.

P. 31, *l.* 30, *for* Thomas David, *r.* Thomas David Rees ; of whom fee p. 27.

P. 32, *l.* 30, *after* country, *r.* " Mr. David Davis, born in the parifh of Whitchurch, and county of Pembroke, 1708; went to America, 1710, took the care of Welfh Tract May 27th, 1748, and continued it till he died in 1769."

P. 33, *l.* 9, from the bottom, *for* Landils *r.* Landilo.

P. 34, *l.* 30, *after* forty, *r.* three. Mr. Rees was paftor at Limehoufe in 1705.

P. 43. *l.* 5, *after* Blaenau, *r.* and Mr. Jofhua James of Abergavenny.

Ibid. *l.* 11, *after* beginning, *r.* fince the Revolution in 1688.

P. 48, *l.* 35, *after* had been in this practice, *r.* and much encouraged it in the Principality.

Ibid. *l.* 36, *after* little, *r.* public.

P. 50, *l.* 12, from the bottom, *dele* a comma before Richard.

P. 55, *l.* 2, *dele* after.

P. 56, *l.* 33, *for* vi. *r.* iii

P. 57, *l.* 41, *for* Devon, *r.* Somerfet.

P. 63, *l.* 29, Rev. Mr. Rowles of Chard, fays, that Mr. William Watkins died before October 1767.

P. 64, *l.* 11, from the bottom, *obferve*, Mr. Watkin Edwards died in 1794, which was after the copy of that fheet was written. There are other inftances in this Tract in which a fimilar remark fhould be made.

Ibid. *l.* 10, from the bottom, *remark*, Mr. Rowles fays, that Mr. Peter Evans died in 1772.

P. 65, *l.* 1. *after* church, *r.* formed, and *for* of, *r.* in, and the fame after Ufk, in the fame line.

Ibid. *l.* 3, put a comma, or femicolon after place; and a, before branch.

P. 67, *l.* 12, *for* Carleon, *r.* Caerleon.

P. 68, *l.* 28, *for* the church, *r.* the Meeting-houfe

P. 73, *l.* 10, *for* Gabriel, *r* George.

P. 74, *l.* 21, 33, 34, *for* Chapel-y-ffm, *r.* Chapel-y-ffin.

P. 75, *l.* 6, 8, from the bottom, *for* Appendix, *r.* Addrefs.

A HISTORY.

OF THE
WELSH ASSOCIATION, &c.

THAT there were Baptists in *England*, in the days of *Henry* the Eighth and before, needs not be proved now: but the fury of persecution was so great in those times, that had they attempted to form a regular Gospel Church, it must have been done without any prospect of its continuance. Therefore this denomination was generally included among those called *Puritans* and *Nonconformists*. But our present concern is chiefly with the principality of *Wales*. It is supposed from circumstances, that a small Baptist Church was formed at *Olchon*, about 1633. If there ever were any written accounts of its regular constitution, it seems they are irrecoverably lost, like many more valuable papers of those times: Mr. *Howell Vaughan*, was the minister there; it is probable he preached mostly among his own small congregation, and not much abroad. After repeated investigations of this subject, it appears that Mr. *Wroth*, Rector of *Llanfaches*, (pronounced *Llanvaches*) in *Monmouthshire*, was the first *Nonconformist* minister in the Principality. It is supposed he began to preach the Gospel, in a very different way from the common clergy, about 1620, or soon after. While he thus preached, and his fame was spreading round the country, Mr. *Walter Cradock*, a young man of a reputable family in that vicinity, then at *Oxford*, and designed for the ministry, coming home to see his friends, and hearing of this remarkable preacher, had the curiosity to go himself to hear him. The consequence was, that he was fully convinced that Mr. *W*'s preaching was right. Not long after, Mr. *Cradock* began to preach the Gospel himself, with life and concern for the salvation of his hearers. Mr. *Wood*, in his *Ath. Oxon.* says, Vol. II. Col. 175, Ed. 2. Mr. *William Erbury*, became student at *Oxford* in 1619, "took one degree in arts, retired into *Wales*, took holy orders, and was there beneficed." But further says, " that he preached in conventicles, and refusing to read the King's declaration for pastimes after divine on the Lord's-day, he was summoned divers times to the high commission court at *Lambeth*, where he suffered for his obstinacy." He then cites a passage out of *Laud*'s Annual Account of his Province for the Year 1634 page 533, which runs thus. " *Landaff* Diocese : The Bishop of *Landaff* certifies, that this year (1634) he visited his Diocese, and found that *W. Erbury*, Vicar of *St. Mary's in Cardiff*, and *Walter Cradock* his Curate, have been very disobedient to his Majesty's instructions, and have preached very schismatically and dangerously to the people. For this he hath given the Vicar a judicial admonition, and will further proceed if he do not submit. As for his Curate *Walter Cradock*, being a bold, ignorant, young fellow, he hath suspended him, and taken away his licence, which he had to serve the Cure."

Mr. *Neale*, in his *History of the Puritans*, Vol. II. Page 253, 275, says, that *Wroth*, and *Erbury*, were cited and summoned to *London*, and there condemned as the chief renders of the church in *Wales*. He says this was done in 1633, and 1635. Thus it appears how the *Rector*, *Vicar*, and *Curate*, were persecuted by *Laud's* influence and approbation, while they were in the establishment; and one of the chief crimes laid to their charge was, refusing to read the declaration for the book of sports on the Lord's-day. Being thus harrassed and troubled, it may be truly said, that they were compelled to leave the Establishment in order to enjoy the liberty of publishing the Gospel in it native simplicity. So they went through the country and preached where they could, in the churches or out, as it happened—where they had hearers there they preached. It does not appear that Mr. *Wroth* went far; he had a gathered church constituted in the parish of *Llanfaches*, in 1639. Some say that Mr. *Erbury* was a considerable itinerant in *Wales*. But the chief of the three was Mr. *Cradock*, he was the youngest, and at that time in his vigor and strength—He preached through *South* and *North Wales* with no small acceptance and success. The author of these papers recollects that when he was young, between the years 1730 and 1740, the aged people among the Dissenters talked much of *Walter Cradock*. Not long after Mr. *Cradock*, Mr. *Vavasor Powell*, another young clergyman began to preach in the same itinerant way: being a popular minister, he was soon persecuted with no small severity. He was a native of *Radnorshire*. These two were University men and able preachers, and were very laborious through the Principality. The former was in sentiments an Independent, and the latter a Baptist.

As yet the people in *Wales* knew little of spiritual things. Mr. *V. Powell*, in his *Brief Narrative*, prefixed to his Bird in the Cage, says, That about 1641, the professors of religion were very few in *Wales*, except in the corners of two or three counties and that about that time a petition was sent to the King shewing, humbly and truly, by many respectable persons, to the King and Parliament, that, upon diligent search, there were scarcely to be found, as many conscientious resident preachers, as there were counties in *Wales*; and that the few who were there, were either silenced or much persecuted. Soon after that, the war broke out, and the country was left, not only without relief, but

the

the few preachers and professors in it were obliged to flee and quit their habitations. Their property was taken away by violence, and their wives and children reduced to great straits. This was the state of the Principality in those afflictive years. It was above fifty years before, that Mr. *John Penry*, a native of *Wales*, and a Baptist, published two Tracts, one to the parliament, and the other to the governors and people of *Wales*, lamenting the ignorance of the people, and how destitute they were of the means of true knowledge. That very year in which he published those tracts, the first *Welsh Bible* that ever was printed, came out in folio, for the churches. The first octavo Bible for the public, came out in 1630, so it was no great wonder that the common people were nearly as ignorant in 1641, as they were in 1588, when Mr. *Penry* published his books. But through all the troubles, and wars of those days, *Cradock* and *Powell*, with a few inferiors, exerted themselves much, and the knowledge of the Gospel greatly increased. Though Mr. *P.* was obliged, by the violence of persecution, to quit the country for a time, yet he returned as soon as things would admit. He had then a testimonial certificate from *London* to *Wales*, signed by eighteen leading ministers, most or all of them Independents or Presbyterians, dated the 11th of September 1646, as related in his life. Though *Powell* and *Cradock* differed in the article of Baptism, yet in doctrine and discipline they agreed heartily in the general, and set up free open communion in *Wales*, maintaining the independency of churches. They both agreed in affection, and exerted themselves much in behalf of their countrymen, and their labor was not in vain in the Lord. Now the light of the Gospel shone so clearly among the people of the country, that they have never since been so dark as they had been long before. Thus the people were united together in a mixed communion consisting of Pædobaptists and Baptists. Though many of the latter were scattered through the country in a few years, yet there were no proper Baptist Churches, except *Olchon* was so, which it is believed was the case.

The first Baptist Church in *Wales*, after the reformation, was formed at *Ilston*, near *Swansea* in *Glamorganshire*, in 1649, which was less than twenty years after the Bible came among the common people in their own language. But we had no account of the formation of this Church, 'till it was given in 1777, by the Rev. Mr. *Isaac Backus*, in his History of *New England*. There we find that Mr. *John Myles*, the Pastor of *Ilston*, left his native country when persecution so raged here, and took the Church Book with him to *New England*, where it is to this day. After that history came out, Mr. *Backus*, being requested to procure a copy of certain parts of Mr. *Myles*'s records, was so very obliging as to send large extracts, written carefully with his own hand. Those manuscripts have been very useful, as will appear below.

✝ Mr. *Myles* seems to have been the first Baptist Minister in *Wales*, who defended and maintained unmixed communion among the

Baptists in the Principality, in a public open way. (*Olchon* minister, of the same sentiment and practice, was a man little known abroad.) After the *Ilston* church was constituted, Mr. *Myles* was very active in other places. This Church Book gives a more particular account of the formation of other churches soon after. From the extracts, we may conclude that the *Hay* church, including *Olchon*, was formed in 1650, as several were baptized in that year at *Llanigon* and the *Hay*; it is probable that they all and *Olchon* made one church formed anew, under the direction of Mr. *Myles*, There were also baptized Brethren, then at *Llanafan*, more of these things follow. The above mentioned extracts shew, ' That members of the two churches of the *Hay* and *Llanafan* assemble at *Ilston*, the sixth and seventh days of the ninth month 1650, who were sent thither by the said churches to the Brethren at *Ilston*, to consult concerning such business as was then by God's assistance determined and expressed as follows.

"The Brethren, previously weighing the great scarcity of ministers that will soundly hold forth the word of truth in *Caermarthenshire*, and the seasonable opportunity now afforded by the Providence of God for the propagation of truth in those parts, do judge that brother *David Davis* shall henceforth endeavour to preach two first days of every two months at *Caermarthen* town or thereabout: and that brother *Myles* shall preach that way one first day in every two months; and that brother *Proser* shall preach there one first day in every two months; and these Brethren are desired to consult and agree among themselves, when it may be most convenient for any one of them to be there. And

"Upon the like serious consideration of the present condition of our Brethren at *Llanafan*, it is by the Brethren here judged convenient, that a constant meeting be there kept by the churches until the Lord shall raise up more able men among themselves, and that bother *David Davis* be desired to be there present as often as he possibly can; but that when he is necessitated to be at *Caermarthen*, then our Brethren of the *Hay* are desired to take care to send, either brother *Proser* or brother *Thomas Watkins*, or some other whom they shall judge convenient."

At the same time it was further agreed, "That these ministers should be assisted by the churches and contributions made for that purpose. For that year it was settled, that each of the three churches should collect ten pounds among themselves, in the whole thirty pounds, and a Brother in each church was there named to take care of that contribution; the first collection to be made as soon as convenient after that agreement, without burdening any of the Brethren." Thus far the business of that meeting.

Now it is supposed that this convention of the messengers of three churches at *Ilston* may claim the honor of being the origin and foundation of the Baptist Association in *Wales*.

The

The extracts give no hint, when or by whom this meeting was appointed, and possibly the records say nothing of that. But it is natural to conclude there were some previous consultations about it. In these few articles we see the very essence and spirit of the Baptist Associations in *Wales* and *England* ever since. The noble design was to assist each other, and to propagate the truth. We have no account who signed these articles, perhaps none then signed. Here we find three Baptist churches formed in 1649 and 1650, and uniting in this friendly connection for mutual comfort and edification. It is at present doubtful whether there was at that time any Association in *England* except the seven churches in and about *London*, who printed the confession of 1643. Be that as it may, it is certain that this was the beginning of general meetings in *Wales*. The appointment of any other meeting at this time is not mentioned in the extracts, yet probably it was done. For they say, "The four churches of *Ilston, Hay, Llanafan,* and *Caermarthen* met at *Caermarthen* the nineteenth of the first month 1651, and appointed some meetings to be at *Gelligâr*. Questions concerning singing psalms and laying on of hands were proposed to be considered by the churches."

Here is a second general meeting, consisting of messengers from four churches. There were not much more than three months between these meetings: the state of the churches required frequent consultations. Here we find *Caermarthen* added as a fourth church, and the Brethren consulting about future meetings at *Gelligâr*, this is the name of a parish in *Glamorganshire*, but near the borders of *Monmouthshire*. The abstracts mention Mr. *David Davis* of *Gelligâr* among those added to *Ilston* church, "From the first of the eight month 1649, to the sixteenth of the same month 1650." Dr. *Walker on the Sufferings of the Clergy*, Part 2 page 228, says, "That Mr. D. *Davis* was chosen to be the minister of the parish of *Kelligar* (this spelling is adopted by several, and may well be used, as it is more ready in *English*) upon certain conditions, by the parishioners, about 1645." So that it seems he was the minister of that parish when he gave himself up as a member at *Ilston*: probably he was baptized when and where he so gave himself a member. The extracts give no information how the above queries were answered, nor whether signed at that meeting, nor when the next was to be, nor any thing of that nature, through the remaining part of 1651 and the whole of 1652.

By loose papers seen at *Abergavenny* about 1752, it appears that in 1651, the churches in *Wales* sent a letter to the Baptist church, meeting at the *Glass-house, Broad-street*, in *London*; giving an account of their state, how they increased and spread; and requesting advice as to the forming of new churches. The answer from *London* then partly transcribed is to this effect. "Regarding the distance of your habitations, we advise, if God hath endowed you with gifts, whereby you may edify one another, and keep up the order and ministry of the church of Christ, you may divide into more particular congregations, but with mutual

A 4   consent

consent; and if their be among you those, who can in some measure take the oversight of you in the Lord, but not else." Then it proceeds to shew and direct them how they might go on to edification. It is signed by *William Conset, William Combey, William Chaffey, Samuel Tull, Edward Green, Joseph Stafford, Robert Cherry, Thomas Carter, John Milamay*, &c.

A church was formed at *Abergavenny*, in 1652, very probable in consequence of the advice from *London*.

The next meeting of which we have any account, was a general meeting of the Elders and others, Messengers of the several churches of *Ilston, Hay, Llantrisaint, Caermarthen*, and *Abergavenny*, holden at *Abergavenny* the fourteenth and fifteenth of the fifth month, 1653. Here *Llantrisaint* occurs, which we had no account of before. This is in *Glamorganshire*, and was formed very probably in 1651 or 1652, after the letter of advice was sent from *London*.

But we have no more account of the church of *Llanafan* in those general meetings for many years. The reason of that silence it is likely may be collected from what follows. Dr. *Walker*, in his *Attempt* on the Sufferings of the Clergy, Part I. page 160, &c. notes, " That in the time of the civil war, *William Williams*, M. A. who served this large parish, was, for some delinquency, ejected by the commissioners, who ordered Mr. *Evan Bowen* to preach in his place at *Llanafan*." This Mr. *Bowen* was a Baptist. The Doctor sneers at him sufficiently; yet confesses that he had been an itinerant, and received a salary on that account: from this it may be presumed, that he was an acceptable minister. In the same parish Mr. *Thomas Evans* was another very acceptable preacher: he also was a Baptist, and a race of very able ministers descended from him. His two sons, *Caleb* and *John*, were worthy ministers in that place; the former in great renown: the late venerable *Hugh Evans* M. A. was his son, and the present truly reverend Dr. *Caleb Evans* is his grandson, and of the fourth generation of very respectable ministers; the two last have been successful pastors of the reputable Baptist church at *Broadmead, Bristol**. Mr. *T. Evans* had his commission to preach, a copy of which is yet preserved, it is dated 16th of May 1653.

Having now such able ministers in the parish, and being so far from the other churches, it seems they rested at home; we hear no more of them in any association with the other churches till the commencement of this century. They are not mentioned in any of the printed narratives of the general assemblies in *London*, 1689, &c.

Now let us return to the general meeting at *Abergavenny*, consisting of the messengers of five churches. The first article in

---

* Besides the four, and Mr *John Evans*, above named, there were and are four more of the same stock in the ministry. Mr. *John Evans* the present pastor at *Pentre*, the same church still, is a grandson to the above Mr. *T. Evans*, and is the last *Evans* of the stock in that country, though there is a numerous issue by females.

the minutes relate to the settling several things in the new church where they met. The advice, we may be sure, was first desired, and then readily given.

The second article runs thus: "We considered the condition of the church at the *Hay*, and upon several complaints made against several disorderly persons, formerly noted, who sought to rent the church, and, as is conceived, to set up themselves as a distinct society, whereby the church is much disturbed and unsettled, which may tend to the dishonour of God and the grief of brethren, and the hindrance of the work of God in the world; it was therefore ordered and concluded,

"1. That a letter be sent to the disorderly brethren, exhorting them to consider from whence they are fallen, and their present practices, and to abstain for the future from uttering rash or scandalous words of the churches, and from receiving into or keeping in their fellowship, such as are, or shall be, cast out by the church, or any that shall irregularly come away from them; and that they attend on the church ministry, not practising in their private meetings any such ordinances as are proper to the church of Christ: and that in case they will not hearken to this our advice, we will at our next meeting, with one consent, declare against and disown them: and withall we desire, that they should at our said meeting give in their reasons unto us, why they charge the church with disorders, and say what the disorders are; where they shall be fully heard, and the business discussed and judged in the fear of the Lord, according to scripture and right reason.

"2. That a letter be sent to the church at the *Hay* to advise them, if they have any fit members, to chuse more Elders to rule and teach that church: and to advise them to submit in the Lord to such as are or shall be chosen Elders among them: that also, if they can, they chuse Deacons in the several parts of the church."

The third and fourth articles are two Queries and Answers.

The fifth article is a consultation and agreement how to supply the *Caermarthen* church with the means of grace for the next half year; and Brother *William Thomas* was appointed to be in or about that town one week in three, for which service he was to receive 10l. to defray his expences; and that church to raise 2l. 10s. of it; *Llantrisaint* 2l. 10s. and *Ilston* 5l. and the *Hay* to assist *Abergavenny* to support Brother *William Prichard*, who was shortly to be sent forth.

Then the conclusion runs thus; "It is also ordered, that the next general meeting be held at *Aberafon* in *Glamorganshire*, upon the seventh day of the seventh month next. Last of all, it is desired that the fourth day come fortnight be set apart by all the churches, as a day of holy rejoicing and praise unto our tender Father, for answering the prayers of his servants, in giving peace to, and preserving it in the poor churches, and for his gracious appearance with us in this our meeting." Then the whole is signed by "*John Myles, David Davis, Walter Prosser, William Thomas, Thomas Proud, Thomas Joseph, Howell Thomas, Leyson Da-*

vis, Stephen Brace, Howell Vaughan, Thomas Watkins, Charles Garſon, Robert Hopkins, Thomas Edwards, Thomas Jones, Thomas Parry, Robert Morgan, Howell Watkins, Thomas Lewis, William Prichard, Anthony Harry, Richard Roſſer, Thomas James, Francis ———." The laſt name is not legible, but is ſuppoſed to be *Giles*.

Here we have twenty-four names. They were now come to a very regular order, and poſſibly they were more ſo before than we have yet found. The narratives of the two former meetings were taken out of the American Extracts. And perhaps they were not full in the Records from whence thoſe were taken. The account of *this* meeting is much abridged in the abſtracts returned from America, though moſt of the names are inſerted, from which it is ſuppoſed that this was the firſt time the meſſengers ſigned the Breviates. The perſons above named were not all miniſters, though probably all meſſengers. Near half of them were in the miniſtry then, or ſoon after, and more than half became aſſiſtants in the miniſtry occaſionally. Some may ſuppoſe that this Aſſociation aſſumed too much authority over the diſturbers of the *Hay* church. But the churches were all young, and circumſtances alter caſes much. The narrative of *this* meeting is taken from the Records of *Abergavenny* church, where it was held.

Here it may be noted, that a new Baptiſt church being formed at *Abergavenny* in 1652, and about ſixty added to it the firſt year or a little more, according to their Records, it rather diſpleaſed ſome Pædobaptiſts that way. This reſpectable meeting ſoon made them more uneaſy. At length, both ſides agreed to have a public diſpute upon the ſubject in *St. Mary's* church in that town, about ſeven weeks after the Aſſociation. The diſputants were *John Tombs*, B. D. Vicar of *Leominſter*; *Henry Vaughan*, M. A. and *John Cragg*, M. A. The former was for Believer's Baptiſm, the two latter for Infant Baptiſm. Mr. *T.* and Mr. *V.* diſputed firſt, then the former with Mr. *Cragg*. Afterwards they all publiſhed on the ſubject. The title of Mr. *C's* publication is, " The Arraignment and Conviction of Anabaptiſm." Mr. *V's* is not large. There is an Epiſtle Dedicatory prefixed, wherein we have theſe words: " Mr. *Tombs* for ſeveral months together, being importuned by letters and meſſengers, came at length to water that which Mr. *Myles*, and Mr. *Proſſer*, and others had planted." Probably this was the firſt public oppoſition of the kind to the Baptiſts in *Wales*.

We ſaw that, by appointment, the next general meeting was to be held on the ſeventh day of the ſeventh month next. But the narrative of that meeting at *Aberafon* ſays, that it was kept on the firſt and ſecond days of the firſt month, 1654. It is in vain for us to inquire how that happened. At this meeting, as in former ones, the common deſign was the edification and comfort of the churches. To that end ſeveral queries were propoſed and reſolved. One query was this: " What are the duties of each of the officers and members in the church?" It is then added, " In order to the anſwering of this queſtion it is deſired that our Brethren, *John Myles*

Myles, David Davis, Walter Proffer, and *William Prichard,* do feverally confider this thing, and certify in writing what they fhall judge concerning it, at our next general meeting." Another minute runs thus: " It is our defire that the church at *Ilfton* do fpare *Brother Myles* as often and as long as they may, to be among the churches of the *Hay* and *Abergavenny,* in order to the fettling of them, and helping them to judge of the feveral gifts of the members among them."

In another article, fupplies were agreed upon for the deftitute church at *Caermarthen,* one week in every four; and the refpective pastors fixed for ten or eleven months to come, in the following order: Meffrs. *William Prichard, William Thomas, Thomas Jofeph, J. Myles, Howell Thomas, D. Davis, W. Proffer, Thomas Jones, Morgan Jones, William Thomas,* and *J. Myles* again. Here are nine public minifters, befides Meffrs. *T. Proud, T. Watkins,* &c. in the four churches.

In confideration of the inability of the church at *Abergavenny* to maintain their minifter comfortably, it was defired that thofe of the *Hay* and *Llantrifaint* would affift.

The church at *Abergavenny* was advifed " to take heed of mixed communion with unbaptized perfons, or any others walking diforderly."

Finally, " In confideration of the ufefulnefs of the general meetings of the Elders and Meffengers of the feveral churches, it was ordered that on the 20th of the feventh month next, there be a meeting at the town of *Lantrifaint,* and fo every half year after, provided, that if there be any extraordinary occafion, then, upon the defire of any of the churches, all the others are to fend their meffengers, to hold fuch a meeting, when need requireth." Then the whole is figned by feventeen names, moft of them the fame as before, and fome new ones; viz. *Hugh Matthews, Griffith Griffith, James Hugh,* and *Thomas Evans. Aberafon* was a branch of *Ilfton* church, which lay then very wide.

The Records fay, that the meeting at *Llantrifaint* was kept on the 30th and 31ft of the fixth month, 1654. Some circumftances occafioned it to be about three weeks before the time appointed. There a query was propofed, concerning laying on of hands. The anfwer was referred to the next meeting; and the Brethren, *J. Myles, D. Davis, William Proffer, W. Thomas,* and *W. Prichard,* appointed " to draw up their judgment from Scripture therein, and the church at *Caermarthen* (which propofed it) was defired, by admonition, &c. to prevent the breaching among them of any thing concerning it, until that meeting be paft " Provifion alfo was made to continue the miniftry there as before.

A query concerning finging Pfalms, was propofed by the church at *Abergavenny.* That likewife was referred to the next meeting; and the Brethren *J. Myles, D. Davis,* and *W. Thomas* defired to ftate the point feverally, according to Scripture.

Another query was, " Whether the faft days, as now appointed, fhould be continued?" The anfwer was, " It is judged, that the appointed faft days fhould be continued; for that it is the agreement of the churches of *England, Scotland, Ireland,* and *Wales,* and our promise to God and them to observe it; and for that, most of the things desired are not yet attained."

At this meeting several articles were considered and settled, respecting the church at *Llantrisaint*; of which one was, that it was advisable they should divide into three parts, and a ministry for each part be supported for their edification; and that their long journies might be spared, &c. Here the answer was given to the query at the last meeting, respecting the several duties of officers and private members. The following is a copy thereof.

" Our Lord Jesus Christ, who is the head of the church, after he had by himself purged our sins, ascended on high, gave gifts to his church, that each joint in the body might have its peculiar gift, and that thereby unity, peace, and order, might be preserved for the good of the whole. Eph. iv. 8, 11, 12, 15, 16.

1. " He gave Apostles, who planted the first churches, and laid down infallible rules of doctrine and discipline, which we are now to observe, in the gathering and building up of churches. Eph. ii. 20, 21.

2. " Prophets, who, by divine inspiration, foretold things to come; as John, &c.

3. " Evangelists, who were the publishers of the Gospel to the world.

4. " Miracles.

5. " Gifts of healing.

6. " Diversities of tongues, for the further publishing and confirmation of the Gospel, by those primitive and extraordinary Apostles, Prophets, and Evangelists. All those offices and gifts were extraordinary, and therefore are now ceased; that being effected whereto they were given, only the three first may be said to remain in their writings; as Luke xvi. 29. and may be said likewise ordinarily to continue, while there are,

1. " Apostles or Messengers sent forth to gather churches out of the world.

2. " Evangelists, or publishers of the glad tidings, which is only some men's special gift.

3 " Prophets, or such as speak to exhortation, &c. of whom hereafter.

" Now there are to continue in the church these officers:

1. " Pastors.

2. " Teachers.

3. " Helps, or those who rule.

" These three are called Elders, Bishops, Watchmen, &c. whose joint office is,

1. " To take care of the church, Acts xx. 17, 28. 1 Pet. v. 2, 3.

2. " To consult on controversies, Acts xv. 1, 2, 6, 23.

3. " To order things in the church, Acts xvi. 4.

4. " To advise in matters of doubt, Acts xxi. 18, 19.

5. " To

5. "To govern, 1 Tim. v. 17. Tit. i. 5.
6. "To visit the sick, if sent for, James v. 14.
7. "To care for the distribution of collections. Acts iv. 37. xi. 29, 30.

"These were the duties of all the Elders, though the greatest charge lay on the Pastors, as appears in that, though there were many Elders in the church at *Ephesus*, yet the epistle in the Revelation the second chapter, is directed but to one, viz. the angel of the church, and the charge given to, and the account required of him wholly. Now more particularly.

"First, The Pastor's office is to do all that tends to the feeding of the flock, Jer. iii. 15. Matt. xxiv. 45. As to

1. "Exhort. Rom. xii. 7, 8. 1 Cor. xii. 8.
2. "Reprove with all authority. Tit. ii. 15.
3. "Cast out. 1 Tim. i. 20. 1 Cor. v. 1, &c.
4. "Lead the sheep.—He is to be the mouth of the whole.
5. "Watch. 2 Tim. iv. 5. Heb. xiii. 17.
6. "Administer all ordinances in the church.
7. "Give himself wholly to the word and doctrine, Acts vi. 4.
8. "Rule well; which consists (1) in the right ordering of questions and disorderly speakings. 1 Cor. xiv. 33, 40. Col. ii. 5, &c. (2) In preserving purity of doctrine and discipline, Rev. chap. ii. and iii. The angels are charged with it.

"Secondly, The Teacher's particular office is, to wait on teaching, to expound scriptures, and confute errors. Tit. ii. 7, 8. 2 Tim. iv. 2, 3. And this is no less the pastor's office.

"Thirdly, The ruling Elder's, or helping office is, to oversee the lives and manners of men: to whom also double honour is due, 1 Tim. v. 17. Rom. xii. 8. He also must take care of God's house, Heb. xiii. 17. 1 Tim. iii. 5.

"Fourthly, The next officer is a Deacon, 1 Tim. iii. 8. who is to serve tables, that is, the Lord's table, and the tables of all others in the church, that shall want his service. He also is to be dedicated to the church's service, as the word *Deacon* imports, Acts vi. 1, &c.

"Fifthly. For the assistance of the Deacons there are widows, of whom, see 1 Tim. v. 16. who are likewise to serve the church, Rom. xvi. 1. most probably in looking to the poor and sick.

"Sixthly. There are, for the further edifying of the church, ordinary prophets, who, though they be not such as wait on the ministry, or are wholly given up to it as yet, are such as being gifted, may speak, as they be permitted, or desired, to edification, exhortation, and comfort, 1 Tim. iv. 15. 1 Cor. xiv. 3, 29, 30.

"Thus far of church-officers with their offices: Now follow the duties of private members, as they are related to their officers and to each other.

"In

" In relation to their Elders, they are to honour them, 1 Tim. v. 17. Submit to and obey them, Heb. xiii. 17. To provide for them, especially such as labour in the word and doctrine, having dedicated themselves thereto, 1 Cor. ix. 7. 1 Tim. v. 8. Gal. vi. 6. To pray for them, Heb. xiii. 18. Col. iv. 3. Eph. vi. 18, 19. Not to grieve them, Heb. xiii. 17. Nor to speak roughly to them, 1 Tim. v. 1. Nor hastily to receive an accusation against them, 1 Tim. v. 19.

" In relation to one another, they are,

" To have and preserve love among themselves, Eph. iv. 1, 2. To strive for the best gifts, especially that they may prophesy, 1 Cor. xiv. 1. Taking heed that they presume not above what is meet, Rom. xii. 3. To admonish, exhort and reprove each other, as in Matt. xviii. 1 Thess. v. 11, 14. To strive to excel in holiness, Heb. xii. 14. More particularly —The rich are not to despise the poor, James ii. 6. But to communicate freely, 1 Tim. vi. 17. Heb. xiii. 16. The poor are not to be idle, nor charge the church unnecessarily, 2 Thess. iii. 11, 12. The young are to honour and reverence the aged, 1 Tim. v. 1, 2. The aged are to be examples to the young. The strong are to bear the infirmities of the weak, and not to offend them in things indifferent, but to respect them, 1 Cor. x. 32. and xii. 23, 24. The weak are not to take upon them the place of Christ in judging their Brethren, who are the servants of Christ, Rom. xiv. 1, 2, &c.

" So in all things, if every one would more carefully follow peace and holiness, and act his own part, there would be no jarrings and divisions, nor yet corporal or spiritual wants, but each member exercising his several gift, the whole body, as the apostle sheweth, being fitly joined together, and compacted by that which every joint supplies, according to the effectual working in the measure of every part, would make increase to the edifying of itself in love." After this,

It was further ordered, " that the proposals which shall be sent, by any particular church, unto any general meeting hereafter, be delivered in writing. And in case there be any matter of controversy, that their arguments be stated, and therewith delivered.

" Ordered, that the next general meeting be held (God willing) at the *Hay*, the last fourth day of the next first month." Then the whole is signed in the manner following,

" The Elders and Messengers of the Church at *Ilston*,

John Myles	*Harry Griffith*
Morgan Jones	*John Davis*
William Thomas	*Hugh Matthews.*
Morgan Jones	

The Elders and Messengers of the Church at the *Hay*.

Walter Prosser   Thomas Watkins.
Charles Garson

The Elders of the Church at *Llantrisaint*.

David Davis   Howel Thomas
Thomas Joseph   Thomas Jones.

The Elders and Messengers at *Abergavenny*.

William Prichard   Richard Rosser
Anthony Harry   Richard Jones.
Thomas James

The Messengers of the Church at *Caermarthen*.

Robert Morgan   Rhydderch Thomas."

Here are twenty one Elders and Messengers of the five Churches, of whom eleven or twelve were ministers then, or soon after, and some of the others a kind of helps.

At this meeting it was agreed to send a copy to each church of the answer to the query regarding the several duties of officers and members.

Here our materials begin to fail. The *Abergavenny* records give no account of any more general meetings than these three; therefore large breviates or minutes of them have been given, by which we may form an opinion of other general meetings, and their business. By these it appears that they were improving every time. The minutes of the *Hay* meeting very probably, are in the *Ilston* book that was carried to *America*.

We have an account of only one general meeting more during that time of liberty. Perhaps that was the chief of all their general meetings from 1650 to 1660. Liberty was not long after that continued. This general meeting was held at *Brecknock*, on the twenty-ninth and thirtieth of the fifth month, 1656. Before this it is probable they had the meeting at the *Hay*, and one or two more. They agreed at this time to publish a Tract, whose title page runs thus, " An Antidote against the infection of the Times; or a faithful *Watch-word* from *Mount Sion* to prevent the Ruin of Souls: whereby some special Considerations are presented to Sinners, Admonitions to Saints, and Invitations to Backsliders.— Published for the good of All, by the Appointment of the Elders and Messengers of the several Churches of *Ilston*, *Abergavenny*, *Tredynog*, *Caermarthen*, *Hereford*, *Bradwardine*, *Cludock*, and *Llangors*, met at *Brecknock* &c." the date as above. Four passages of scripture are added as mottos. " *London*: Printed for *T. Brewster*, at the three Bibles, at the West End of St. Paul's, 1656."

This

This tract contains fifty-five pages small quarto, close printed: it is a home, affectionate address to the three characters mentioned above. In that to sinners, p. 16. it is noted. "That since the enjoyment of precious liberty, to hold forth the word of God to poor straying souls, many thousands are come to the profession of the Gospel; and particularly the poor country wherein we live, may for ever bless the Lord, and remember with thankfulness all such as were instruments for the good of their souls, in procuring the much envied, and too short-lived act for the propagation of the Gospel in *Wales*, whereby many stumbling-blocks were removed out of the way, and the true and faithful servants of Jesus Christ encouraged to preach the Gospel with freedom and countenance, and so in a few years such a change is wrought, even in the darkest places, that it is wonderful to behold what abundance of heavenly wisdom and grace hath, through the preaching of the Gospel, been poured into the hearts of thousands of poor ignorant straying people."

Here it may be noted, that in 1649, there was a complaint made to parliament, that the inhabitants of the Principality of *Wales* were destitute of the means of christian knowledge, their language was little understood, their clergy ignorant and idle; so that the people had hardly a sermon once in a quarter of a year; and were destitute both of bibles and catechisms.—The parliament took these things into consideration, and on February 22, 1649-50, an act passed for the better propagation and preaching of the Gospel in *Wales*—and to continue for three years. Commissioners were then appointed to eject ignorant and scandalous ministers, and to place others in their room. Of these things, see *Neale's* History of the Puritans, vol. 4. page 15, 116, &c. This act for the propagation of the Gospel was procured by the influence of Messrs. *Vavasor Powell*, *Jenkin Jones*, &c. Many spoke and wrote against it, and many for it. But the benefit of it continues to this day, short as it was in duration.

As yet we have found no account of any other general meeting in *Wales*, after this of 1656, till the revolution: it is very probable there were several after that before 1660, but some notice should be taken of the number and names of the churches at this meeting: we had but five in the three preceding meetings, but eight in this, and in the latter but three of the former five. How can a stranger account for this? It seems, that publication entitled *An Antidote*, &c. was designed before-hand, in vindication of the Baptists, so much then spoken of and written against. Mr. *Richard Harrison* was a noted popular Baptist minister, at *Hereford*, probably he was at *Brecknock* by desire, so *Hereford* is named though not in *Wales*; nor in the connection. The *Hay* is not named, but *Cludock* and *Bradwardine*, two branches of that church are. It seems by this time, that they were uncomfortable at the *Hay*, and Mr. *Walter Prosser* gone from them and settled at *Tredynock*, not far from *Llantrisaint*, in

Mon-

Monmouthshire, for he is named by *Dr. Calamy* as ejected from that place a few years after. It seems *Mr. Proffer* was at *Brecknock*, therefore that place is named. *Llangors* was a branch of *Abergavenny*, or perhaps *Mr. John Edwards*, a member of that church, was then settled by the commissioners at *Llangors*; so he being at *Brecknock*, the place might be named on that account. For some reason *Llantrisaint* was not named at *Brecknock*: we may be confident this is near the truth, if not quite. The Baptists in that time of their infancy, as separate churches in *Wales*, were considerably under the scourge of the tongue. The pen and the press were employed against them, as appears by the preface of the above antidote. *Mr. Cragg's* large and virulent book, on the subject of Baptism, came out this year. And the people called *Quakers*, particularly *John Moon*, and some of his friends, printed papers about this time against the Baptists in *Radnorshire* and *Llanafan*, and those on the border of *Montgomeryshire*. *Mr. Backus* in his history, (vol. i. p. 460.) informs us, that the Baptist churches in *Wales*, gathered by *Mr. Myles* and others, published a confession of their faith, which was publickly opposed by *George Fox* the Quaker. So they had a loud call for the *antidote*. A sight of that confession of faith would be very gratifying *; but the *Brecknock* tract is a good evidence of the orthodoxy of our brethren in those early days.

This is the last account we have of the association in the time of the COMMONWEALTH. Very probably it continued for three or four years longer; but the restoration of *Charles* II. in 1660, soon put an end to the liberty of the Nonconformists; and the tyranny which followed hindered their associating for about thirty years, till the GLORIOUS REVOLUTION opened the way, near the close of 1688.

Of the Elders and Messengers named above (page 14, 15.) the following were ministers then, or afterward: *John Myles, Morgan Jones, William Thomas, Morgan Jones, Walter Proffer, Thomas Watkins, David Davies, Thomas Joseph, Howell Thomas, Thomas Jones, William Prichard, Anthony Harry, Robert Morgan* and *Thomas Proude*. The last is not there named; it seems he was absent from the association at *Llantrisaint* in 1654, but he was a kind of colleague to *J. Myles*. Several of these were set in parish churches by the commissioners, instead of incapable ministers. The following are named by *Dr. Calamy*, in his *Abridgement*, among the ejected ministers. *J. Myles, Thomas Proude, Howell Thomas, Thomas Joseph, Morgan Jones, David Davies*, and *Walter Proffer*. These seven belonged to the association, unless *David Davies* might be another of the name. The following are also among the ejected, who were not in the association: *Jenkin Jones, Mr. Abbot, Mr. Milman, Watkin Jones* (said by *Dr. Walker* to be

---

* To the Author of this History.

an Anabaptist, but some Pædobaptists say he was not,) *Henry Williams* and *Vavasor Powell*. These were zealous ministers, and all Baptists, unless we except Mr. *Watkin Jones*, who was an active, useful man. Above (see page 14.) there are two of the name of *Morgan Jones* mentioned at *Llantrisaint*, as messengers from *Ilston*; but Dr. *Calamy* mentions only one. Yet Dr. *Walker*, in his Sufferings of the Clergy, part IId. p. 338. mentions a *Morgan John* succeeding *Theodore Price* at *Laleston*, &c. in *Glamorganshire*. It seems he was the second of the two; a learned man, and an ancestor to the Rev. Mr. *Morgan Jones*, now of *Hammersmith*, near *London*; Dr. *W.* says he was an Anabaptist. Probably he died before the ejection, so could not be in Dr. *Calamy*'s list. Dr. *Walker*, part I. p. 160. says, that *Anthony Harry* was allowed by the commissioners to preach at, and receive the profits of, *Llanvihangel*; from which place *John Griffith*, *A. M.* had been ejected. He was a member of *Abergavenny;* received by letter from *Llantrisaint*. Probably he died before the *Bartholomew* ejection. Mr. *John Edwards* was mentioned above * as settled at *Llangors*. Messrs. *Thomas Evans* and *Evan Bowen*, have been named before †. We know not what were the sufferings of the latter, nor when he died. The former was an ejected minister, though not mentioned in Dr. *Calamy*'s account. He lived, preached and suffered, from the Restoration to the Revolution; was a truly worthy servant of Christ, and died in 1688. Mr. *Hugh Evans* was a truly laborious, acceptable Baptist minister in *Radnorshire*, from 1646 to about 1656, when he finished his course. *John Moon* called him " a blind priest in *Wales*;" but the deceased man's character was well defended in print, in 1658, by *John Price* and *William Bound*. Messrs. *Francis Giles* and *Thomas Parry* were also named before ‡. They weathered out all the persecution from 1660 to 1688. Dr. *Christopher Price* was in the ministry about 1650, or soon after; of him more below. *Henry Gregory* and *Lewis Thomas* entered on their ministry at the beginning of the persecution, or perhaps a little before.

Thus it appears that there were near *thirty* Baptist ministers in *Wales* in the time of the COMMONWEALTH; and that most of them lived to the restoration, and felt the bitterness and fierceness of the persecution that followed. There were besides several assistants, and occasional exhorters, not named here.

Of Mr. *J. Myles*, his removal with several of his friends to *America*, his forming a church at *Rehoboth*, his usefulness at *Boston*, in *New England*, &c. and his death in 1683, see *Backus*'s History, where an excellent account is given of him. Dr. *Cotton Mather*, as quoted by *Crosby*, speaks very honour-

* Page 17.   † Page 8.   ‡ Page 10.

ably of him. Dr. *Calamy* only fays, that he was an Anabaptift, and went to *New England*.

Mr. *Thomas Proude*, a good man, one of the ejected minifters, is named properly in the firft edition of Dr. *Calamy's* Abridgement. It was probably through careleffnefs that his name was printed *Froude* in the fecond edition: *Crofby* and Mr. *Palmer* have followed the erroneous copy. Dr. *Calamy* only fays of him " an Anabaptift."

Mr. *Jenkin Jones* was very active, ufeful, refpectable, and much of the gentleman. He was called *Captain Jones*, and had been in the army. It is faid, that as he was once going to preach, a perfon way-laid him, with a refolution to kill him; but coming up to him, he was fo ftruck with the comelinefs and majefty of his perfon, that his fpirit failed, and he went to hear him, and was much affected with the fervice. Dr. *Calamy* calls him a Catabaptift: though he fays, that he had been brought up at *Oxford*, was a preacher before the war, took pains in feveral counties, was imprifoned, &c. We know not when or where he finifhed his courfe.

Mr. *Walter Proffer* ftands in our lift above *. He continued a laborious, worthy minifter. We have no account of the time of his death. Dr. *Calamy* only juft names him.

Meffrs. *Howel Thomas*, *Thomas Jofeph* and *Morgan Jones*, of *Lanmadack*, are mentioned by Dr. *Calamy*, as ejected in *Glamorganfhire*. He treats them all with contempt, but does not fay that they were Anabaptifts. But Dr. *Walker* fpeaks out, that H. *Thomas* and T. *Jofeph* were Anabaptifts. Dr. *Calamy* fays, that the latter was an ingenious hufbandman, but an ignorant preacher; and yet Dr. *Walker* calls him a fhoemaker

Of Mr. *William Thomas*, fomething was faid above †. Dr. *Calamy* hath two of the name; one in *Glamorganfhire*, and the other in *Carmarthenfhire*: he ftyles the latter an itinerant Probably he was our *William Thomas*, as he preached fo often about *Carmarthen*; but it feems he died in *Monmouthfhire*, as an old book, in that county, contains this manufcript note: " *William Thomas*, a preacher of the true Word of God, de- " parted this life the 26th of July, 1671, and was buried at " *Llantrifaint*." Another manufcript account fays, that Mr. *Walter Proffer* was eminent in the miniftry, and preached often at *Llantrifaint* to W. *Thomas's* people; by this it feems that the former furvived the latter.

Of Mr. *David Davies's* activity and fervices, fome account is given above ‡. What became of him in the perfecuting times does not appear; nor when he died.

Mr. *Abbot* is faid, by Dr. *Calamy*, to have been ejected from *Abergavenny*. He was a Baptift. The relation of the

* Page 15. † Page 9. ‡ Pages 6, 7, 9--11.

conference

conference at *Abergavenny* *, in 1653, fays, page 29. " *Mr.* " *Abbets (Abbot)* preacher, refident there; one who had " been dipped, being in the pulpit with *Mr. Tombs*, ftood " up and faid, &c." *Mr. Crofby* names a *Mr. Abbot*, the firft of five gentlemen of learning, who, he fays, left the eftablifhment and joined the Baptifts †.

Mr. Vavafor Powel was exceeding laborious and ufeful in *Wales*, and a great fufferer. He died a prifoner in the *Fleet*, 1671, and was buried in *Bunhill-fields, London*. His life was printed not long after.

Mr. Henry Williams is named by *Dr. Calamy* among thofe ejected in *Montgomeryfhire*; the Doctor gives him a very good character, but hints nothing of his being a Baptift. " He died about 1685, aged about 60."‡ His fufferings were great.

Mr. Thomas Jones, the 4th elder at *Llantrifaint* §, probably fettled with a branch of that people, which met at, and about *Kelligar*, ~~and regularly formed into a church in 1654, in confequence of agreement and advice at that meeting~~. There were fome gentlemen of property and influence in that church. By writings and circumftances, it is conjectured that he died about 1675. Thus we have about twenty Baptift minifters in *Wales*, who *ended their days* before 1689; moft of them, if not all, men " of whom the world was not worthy."

The following minifters, of the fame perfecuted denomination, bore their teftimony thro' all the hardfhips from 1660 to 1688. *Meffrs. Henry Gregory, Thomas Parry, Thomas Watkins, Chriftopher Price, William Prichard, Francis Giles, Thomas Quarrel, William Milman, Lewis Thomas, Robert Morgan*, and *John Edwards*. and Thomas Evans.

Dr. Calamy names *Mr. William Jones*, as ejected in *Carmarthenfhire*. He was wrong *informed* regarding the name of the place; or the name was wrong *printed*. When *Mr. William Jones* was ejected, he was an Independent. Some time after the ejectment, he was taken and caft into *Carmarthen* caftle for preaching.

In that confinement, he, and fome of his fellow-prifoners, had feveral converfations upon baptifm. The confequence was, that he was fecretly perfuaded, in his own mind, that believers baptifm was the real Scripture one. But he kept his conviction to himfelf while in prifon. After he was liberated, he was determined to anfwer a good confcience; he took his journey to the valley of *Olchon*, the church in that place being reputed both very ancient and regular, and there he was baptized; probably by *Mr. Thomas Watkins*. He returned home, informed a few friends what he had done,

---

* See page, 10. † Crofby, vol. iv. p. 251. ‡ Calamy's Account, p. 712. § Mentioned in page 15th of this Hiftory.

and

and gave his reasons for it. This, it is supposed, was about 1665 or 1666.

Be it noted here, that hitherto the Baptists were in the *eastern* side of *South Wales*, except a few about *Carmarthen*, and they were in mixed communion with independents, not only in the two churches in the counties of *Montgomery* and *Denbigh*, but in most, if not all, of our congregations in *Wales*.

It was not long till *Mr. Jones* began to baptize. In 1668 a church was formed on the borders of the counties of *Pembroke* and *Carmarthen*. The constituents were thirty-three. *Mr. Thomas Watkins* of *Olchon*, and *Mr. William Prichard* of *Abergavenny*, assisted in forming it. *Mr. W. Jones* was soon chosen the Elder of it, and other officers were appointed in proper time. Of this church called *Rushacre* more below.

When liberty of conscience passed into a law, early in 1689, the bowels of the *London* ministers yearned over their brethren in the country, who had been so long in the storms and tempests of persecution, and they wished to learn their conditions. Hence they sent a circular letter through *England* and *Wales*, dated July 28, 1689, inviting the churches to send Elders and Messengers to a general meeting in *London*, on the 3d of *September* ensuing. The time was rather short; however about one hundred and fifty met, from about an hundred churches. The following Messengers from *Wales* were present: from *Pembrokeshire*, *William Jones*, Pastor; and *Griffith Howell*. The names of several of the places in the printed narratives of that meeting are wrong. All the places mentioned in *Wales* are wrong spelt, except *Swanzey*, so spelt then, it seems, and so still the place in *America*, where *Mr. J. Myles* settled: *Monmouthshire*, *William Prichard*, Pastor, *Christopher Price*, Minister; *Swanzey*, ~~Lewis Thomas~~, Pastor, *Francis Giles*. Here we have six ministers from *Wales* in the general meeting in *London*. The business of that assembly was too copious to be here inserted*. Among many important things, they agreed to set forth a *Confession of Faith*; and thirty-eight of the ministers signed their approbation of it, in behalf of the whole assembly, among whom were *Christopher Price* and *William Prichard* from *Wales*. Let this suffice for the year 1689. We proceed to,

1690. The general meeting was in *London*, the 9th of *June*, this year. The printed narrative of that meeting does not give the names of the ministers then present, only of twenty who signed the General Epistle, or Circular Letter to the churches; nineteen from the several parts of *England*, and *William Prichard* from *Wales*. One particular business of that meeting was, to divide the churches in the several parts of *England* and *Wales*, into proper, convenient associations. The churches in *South Wales* were formed into one association, and

---

* It may be seen in the Baptist Register, Part the Ist, 1790. EDITOR.

they go under these names in the Narrative, *Langon, Bergavenny, Llanwanarth, Blainegwant, Golchon, Craig-yr-allt, Lanvabon, Ynys-vach, Rushacre,* and *Lanydwr.* *Ilston* was left out, now called *Swansea*. A stranger might suppose these to be ten or eleven churches; but they were no more than six. The three last were only so many places where the same church met to worship for many years. *Craig-yr-allt* and *Llanfabon* were two places where *Kelligar* church commonly met, and *Llangwm* was the former *Llantrisant* church, and *Dr. Price* became one of their Pastors, and several members of *Abergavenny* joined them. *Llanwenarth* is about two miles west of *Abergavenny,* and a church was formed there, branching to *Blaenau, Llangors,* &c. *Swansea,* as we have said, was omitted.

Dr. *Christopher Price* was a gentleman of property, near *Abergavenny.* He was brought up at first to physic and surgery, so went by the title of *Doctor.* He was a very worthy character. Two papers yet preserved, in his own hand-writing, contain an account of the *Welsh* churches this year. One paper is a rough draft, the other the fair copy sent to the General Assembly in London. They are not the same *verbatim,* but both afford more light than one. He begins with his own church. In one paper, he says, it met at *Llangwm* and *Abergavenny*; in the other, at *Llantrisaint* and *Abergavenny,* of course they met in the three places. The church consisted of about eighty members, scattered as wide as twenmiles. Brother *Quarrel* was the other Pastor, but he presided iefly at *Llantrisaint* and *Langwm,* and Brother *Price* at *Abergavenny*; the former had to assist him, Brother *William Milman* and Brother *Walter Williams*; the latter had Brother *Nathaniel Morgan*. Brother *Robert Jones* also assisted in the church. Brother *John Edwards* also is named as an ancient faithful disciple. Mr. *Nathaniel Morgan* was a gentleman of property and repute. His daughter was mother to the present Dr. S. Stennett. Mr. *Quarrel* is mentioned by Dr. *Calamy* among the ejected ministers as at *Owestry*; and Mr. *Palmer* adds, that he was the first pastor of the congregational church at *Shrewsbury,* in *Oliver's* time, and afterwards preached there as often as the violence of the times would permit. It is supposed the church at *Shrewsbury* were Baptists, with, perhaps, a few Independents among them. Mr. *Quarrel* was a *North Wales* man. He lived to a great age, about twenty years after the Revolution. His house at *Llangwm* is known still.

Dr. *Price* calls *Llanwenarth* and *Blaenau* two congregations, though as yet but one church. The members at the former place about eighty, at the latter about thirty. Brother *William Prichard* Pastor; *Francis Giles, David James, John Spencer* and *Morgan William,* assistants.

Olchon

Olchon, about thirty members; Brother *Thomas Watkins* Paſtor, and *Brother Thomas Parry* aſſiſting. This is a great decreaſe ſince 1654, when they laid ſo wide; but perſecution and quarrels made ſad work. It ſeems the Doctor does not reckon *Llanigon* in this account, and fixes the numbers every where rather by gueſs.

Craig-yr-allt, about fifty or ſixty members, no Paſtor; ſome gifted brethren; their names not mentioned. Ordinances adminiſtered by Brother *Lewis Thomas*, and Brother *Robert Morgan*, alternately; they had a long way to come from *Swanſea*, where they were paſtors. This church in a thriving condition; hearers numerous and many members lately added.

Swanſea, Brother *Lewis Thomas*, and Brother *Robert Morgan*, Elders.

Pembrokeſhire, Brother *William Jones*, and Brother *Griffith Howell*, Elders. This was the *ſixth* church.

He mentions two other ſmall congregations in one of the papers, but they were only branches of the above church. *Ed.*

This account to *London* was intended to ſhow what miniſters were in ſtrait circumſtances, that they might receive ſome aſſiſtance from the fund. A letter * from *Dr. Price* to *Mr. Iſaac Marlow*, one of the treaſurers, intimates that the latter had written to the former to deſire the account. The Doctor there ſays, that formerly he had procured from *Brother Woollaſton* ‡, at ſeveral times, four or five hundred pounds for poor miniſters, but had then received nothing from him for five years paſt; yet had obtained ſome ſmall ſums from charitable perſons in *London*, for the purpoſe. In another letter he ſays, that he had been forty years in the miniſtry, but had received nothing for his labour therein; nay, that he aſſiſted others often, which no doubt was the caſe.

From the identical letters † which the churches or congregations at *Blaenau, Llanwenarth, Olchon,* and *Craig-yr-allt.* ſent to the aſſembly in *London* 1690; it appears they were five churches ſtill as in 1655, with this difference, *Olchon* inſtead of *Hay*; *Llanwenarth* inſtead of *Abergavenny*; *Llantriſaint*, as before, but *Langwm* and *Abergavenny* branches of it; *Swanſea* inſtead of *Ilſton*; *Craig-yr-allt*, a new church, and *Carmarthen* diſſolved; the remaining members joined to *Swanſea* church, which laid very wide.

The church in *Radnorſhire* and *Llanafan* makes the *ſeventh*. They had left the aſſociation, as noted above. And probably the Circular Letter from *London* in 1689, did not reach them. As they are not in the *London* narratives, we may conclude they ſent no meſſengers thither. But they were ſtill a repuꞏtable people. M. *T. Evans* was lately dead, as obſerved before, but the venerable Mr. *Henry Gregory* was ſtill alive. Here

---

* In the poſſeſſion of *Mr. Thomas*. † Mr. *Thomas* has them.
‡ Who was *Brother Wollaſton?* Editor.

it should be noted, that about 1683, or 1684, some of the members of this church emigrated to *Pennsylvania*, and in January 1687-8, with a few more, formed the first Baptist Church in that province, of which one of them, Mr. *Samuel Jones*, in time became the minister. He was a very benevolent, active, solid, man, and of great use to that church in its infancy. From that small company sprung two or three Baptist Ministers in *America*, particularly that great character the late *Rev. Isaac Eaton, M. A.* whose name will be precious for ages. Indeed, many went from *Wales* to *Pennsylvania* * ; and a considerable number of the first constituents of the original churches beyond the Atlantic emigrated from the Principality.

1691. In the *London* Narrative of this year, *Christopher Price* is among the seventeen who signed the epistle to the churches. Whether any one else from *Wales* attended at that general meeting, we cannot say. There we have the churches in *Wales* named pretty nearly the same as in 1690, but much better than in 1689; they were now divided into two associations; those in the *east* to form one, and the *Pembrokeshire* church, meeting in three different places, to form the other. Let us proceed to

1692. This year the GENERAL ASSEMBLY in LONDON, considering the distance, expense, and inconvenience of travelling far, agreed to divide the LONDON Association, so to have one in *London*, as before, and one at *Bristol*, to meet at different times of the year, and keep up mutual fellowship and correspondence. This was to ease persons at a distance. In the Narrative of 1692, places and ministers are printed, as in 1689, but some of the blunders in the one are corrected in the other; yet not those which belong to the Principality. One of the six former ministers is omitted, the other five as before. The brethren of the Principality, in future, were to attend at *Bristol*, it being nearer for them.

1693. The *Western General Meeting* was at *Bristol*, according to appointment. Among the eighteen who signed the Circular Letter this year are, *George John*, or *Jones*, and *James James*. These were both from the *Pembrokeshire* church. The reader may not be displeased here with the following short digression:

It was observed above, that this church was constituted in 1668, being the midst of the persecuting time. But through all they did not only live, but thrive. In future years, it acquired the title of THE COLLEGE, as it produced so many valuable ministers. On a perusal of their records, their state in 1689, will be found thus: their number of members one hundred and thirteen; that is, eighty more than at their first forma-

---

* See *Mr. Edwards's* Materials towards a History of the Baptists in *Pennsylvania*. p. 6, &c. and p. 16. Printed in 1770.

tion, being then about thirty-three, fifteen of whom were yet alive. These one hundred and thirteen resided in thirty-eight parishes, with this exception, that a few of the parishes were in two counties, viz. fifty-nine in *Pembrokeshire*, thirty-five in *Carmarthenshire*, and nineteen in *Cardiganshire*. Among these there were eleven in the ministry; some of whom had laboured long, and suffered much; others were just entering on the work: their names were, *William Jones, Griffith Howell, George Jones, James James, Thomas David Rees, Thomas Griffiths, Evan David, John Jenkins, Richard Williams, John David*, and *Samuel Jones;* and, soon after, *Morgan Griffiths*, if he had not then begun to preach. These twelve were not occasional helpers merely, but ministers of note, who wore well to the last, as will appear concerning several of them below.

After this, liberty being established, the denomination spread still wider. This raised opposition from the Pædobaptists, particularly the Independents. After several debates, both sides agreed to preach upon baptism at *Pen-y-lan*, in *Pembrokeshire*. Mr. *John Thomas*, the Independent minister, preached first on infant baptism; Mr. *John Jenkins*, pastor of the church at *Rushacre*, on a future day, preached on believer's baptism. The consequence was, that many of the Independents were soon after baptized. This was in 1692. This affair so alarmed the Pædobaptists, that they applied to Mr. *Samuel Jones*, of *Glamorganshire*, to defend the subject; but he declining it, his former pupil Mr. *James Owen*, then at *Oswestry, Shropshire*, undertook it. In 1693, his book came out, entitled, *Infant Baptism from Heaven*, printed in the language of the country. This, it is thought, was the first tract on infant baptism that appeared in *Welsh*. It was also turned into *English*. Mr. B. *Keach* published an answer to it, which was translated into *Welsh*, and also *Norcott's* Book on the subject; so that the Baptists lost no ground.

1694 and 1695. Here it may be observed, that, hitherto the friends in the Principality had met to worship in private houses, and shifted as they could. In 1695, a very convenient meeting-house was built at *Llanwenarth*. The land was given by *Dr. Price*, in a lease of two hundred years; at the expiration of which, it was to return to the right heir. This was the first place erected by our denomination in the Principality. About this time died the venerable *Thomas Watkins* of *Olchon*, who had served the church with great reputation for about fifty years, and left a very honourable character behind him.

1696. At the general meeting at *Bristol* this year, there was a Query from *Wales* which ran thus:

" Whether it be lawful for an orderly gospel church to divide by general consent, into two, or more churches, for the sake of edification, when the members live far asunder, and are perhaps numerous?" The answer was in the affirmative, thus:

"That which is adapted to promote the glory of God, and the good of souls, should be done, *Phil.* iv. 8. And it is evident that these things are so; as church members hereby better answer the end of communion, and keep the order and the discipline of Christ more to his praise, their mutual edification, and the spreading of the Gospel. But care should be taken to have ministers in each part, and each part should be sufficient to keep up church order."

In this case, the assembly gave these directions.

1. To write down the names of the members of the whole church, and the part to which each chuse to join.

2. To keep a day of public fasting in each part, where there shall be a minister, or where ministers and people are called and gathered together. Then to make their consent public, with supplications to God for his presence and blessing. Then to give instructions and exhortations to the parties suitable to the occasion, that they may behave as the church of Christ. This should be done, in one part, by the elder of the other part, or rather by one belonging to another church.

This year the *Blaenau* church was constituted, probably according to the above advice and direction. Their first Pastor was *Mr. Abel Morgan*, of whom more hereafter. They had been a branch of *Llanwenarth* about thirty-five years.

We suppose it was this year likewise, that *Glandwr* church was formed, according to the same advice and direction. This had been many years a distant branch of the *Pembrokeshire* church, and wrongly called *Llanydwr*. The elders of this new church were *Thomas David Rees* and *James James*, who both lived among them. There were now *eight* churches in *Wales*, and *Radnorshire* made the *ninth*.

1697. This year died the great and worthy *Dr. C. Price*, who had, for about fifty years, laid out himself zealously and honourably in the cause of Christ, and his afflicted people. Through the long *persecution* he readily relieved the distressed, and eased many in their straits, not only of his own denomination, but other persecuted and oppressed Dissenters.

1698. Our brethren from *Wales* still continued to attend the *Western annual meeting*, which was this year at *Taunton*; but by reason of their distance from the different parts of *Somerset* and *Devon*, where it was sometimes kept, the expense of travelling, and many other inconveniences, they earnestly wished to have an Association among themselves: nor does it appear that they much attended the associations appointed in 1690 and 1691.

1699. This year a new church was constituted at *Trosgoed* (now *Maes-y-berllan*) four or five miles north east from *Brecknock*,

nock. The conftituents were fome from *Llanwenarth* and *Llangors*, and fome who had been in communion with Independents, &c. Their firft Paftor, Mr. *Richard Williams*, from *Pembrokeſhire*, was named above *. *Olchon* not having been fettled with a paftor fince the death of Mr. *T. W.* the new and old church defired Mr. *R. Williams* to take the paftoral care of both. He complied, and the two churches, and alfo *Llanigon* included, united during his life. A very large and laborious charge, but he attended it cheerfully, and filled his office with great fatisfaction.

This alfo was the laft year the friends from the Principality travelled over the water. The weftern meeting was at *Taunton* again this year. The *Blaenau* records contain the breviates of thofe meetings at *Briftol*, &c. to 1699; and then add, " Now " follow the affairs of the WELSH ASSOCIATION." The Meffengers from *Wales* had attended in *London* four years, and at *Briftol* and *Taunton* feven years; eleven in all.

1700. The Affociation was at *Llanwenarth*, on the fixth of the third month *May*. Our denomination then began the year on the firft of *March*. Here were thirteen Queries propofed and anfwered judicioufly and fcripturally; but moft of them refpected church difcipline. About this time died thefe three worthies;

1. Mr. *William Jones*, the father of the weftern churches in *Wales*: he fuffered much, and was imprifoned at *Carmarthen* and *Haverfordweft*, yet was in great repute among the gentlemen of both counties. He laboured, but not in vain in the Lord, as will appear in thefe papers.

2. Mr. *Thomas David Rees*, he lived in *Cardiganſhire*, and had very confiderable property; he was eminent for his hofpitality; a great ſhelter in the *Glandwr* part of the church; and his memory was long precious.

3. The venerable M*r*. *Henry Gregory*, in *Radnorſhire*. He likewife had honourably weathered through all the perfecution from the Reftoration to the Revolution. He kept a fmall farm to fupport his family. He was fined, and his cattle taken away, but he lived and died in great repute.

About 1700, Mr. *Morgan Griffiths*, named before, became Paftor of the church at *Craig-yr-allt*, which had been without a Paftor for about twenty-five years. They were ferved monthly by *Meffrs. Lewis Thomas*, and *Robert Morgan*, alternately; and other gifted brethren fupplied the reft of the time.

1701. The meeting was again at *Llanwenarth*. The account of the bufinefs of the meeting is thus introduced: " Queries propofed and refolved at a general meeting of the " minifters, elders, and meffengers of the feveral churches, " under believers baptifm, and laying on of hands, at *Llan-*

* See page, 25.

wenarth

"wenarth, the ninth and tenth days of the fourth month called *June* 1701."

The Queries are twenty-four in number, all upon discipline, several of them pleasing; a few suited to those times; and some referred to the discretion of the respective churches. It is probable all the churches had copies of the Queries and Answers, instead of a Circular Letter. It does not appear that sermons were yet introduced at the associations in *England* or *Wales*. The time was spent in prayer, and consultation, how to promote the interest of the churches. The answers to the Queries here were signed by *Lewis Thomas, William Prichard, John Jenkins, Robert Morgan, Richard Williams*, and *Abel Morgan*. All worthy names. Probably more ministers attended, though these only signed. The next meeting appointed to be at *Swansea*, on Tuesday in the Whitsun-week, 1702.

In this year, 1701, a decent agreeable meeting-house was built for the *Pembrokeshire* church. Upon a stone on the inside of the building, a *Welsh* inscription was set; in *English* thus; "This house was erected at the charge of *John Evans* of *Llwyndwr*, in the year 1701, for the use of the people who hold the six principles in Heb. vi. 1, 2." Mr. *John Evans* was a gentleman of estate, and considerable property; remarkably generous and hospitable. The meeting-house was called *Rhydwilim*, by which name we shall now call the church. This was the *second* Baptists meeting-house in *Wales*.

This year was also remarkable for the emigration of sixteen members, with their families and friends, from the churches at *Glandwr* and *Rhydwilim* to *Pennsylvania*. One of the sixteen was Mr. *Thomas Griffiths*, a minister named above. Mr. *Morgan Edwards*, in his Materials, calls this, "a church emigrant." This company found out good Mr. *S. Jones*, and company, who had settled near twenty years before, and were settled at *Pennepeck*, now *Lower Dublin*. From thence Mr. *Thomas Griffiths* and company removed, and having formed themselves into a regular church, they settled at a place which they called *Welsh Tract*. Two more of the sixteen turned out successive Pastors of that church. This was the *second* Baptist church in *Pennsylvania*.

1702. A letter from one of the churches to this association expresses their joy, that the general meeting in *Wales* was again revived and raised from the grave of oblivion; and mentions the usefulness of such meetings, &c.

The Circular Letter this year begins thus: "The Elders, "Ministers, and Messengers, met in association at *Swansea* "the 26th and 27th of the third month, 1702. To the "several churches to whom we relate, viz. *Llanwenarth*, "*Aberystryth*, *Olchon*, *Radnor*, *Felindre*, *Newhouse*, *Llanon*, "and the brethren in the *Moor*,—greeting."

Here

Here the names are different from thofe which are given
above; but the whole may be eafily reconciled thus: *Swanfea*
is not named in the addrefs; *Llanon* and the *Moor* were two
diftant branches of *Swanfea*. Thefe formed two churches
many years after, as will appear below. *Aberyftryth* is the
name of the parifh where the *Bleanau* church met. *Felindre*
is the name of another place, where *Glandwr* church met.
The *Newhoufe* was *Rhydwilim*. *Radnorfhire*, now joined the
affociation. So here were properly but feven churches. *Llantrifaint* and *Craig-yr-allt*, are not mentioned among them. Poffibly it was an omiffion ; or, perhaps, they fent no Meffengers
this year. The Letter thanks the focieties for fending their
Meffengers; mentions peace in the churches, the judgments
of God abroad, the wars in *Germany*, &c. A day of folemn
fafting was appointed. The next affociation to be at *Llanwenarth*, on *Tuefday* and *Wednefday* in the Whitfun-week: the
firft day to be fpent in fafting and prayer, and a fermon on
that day; the fecond day to anfwer queries, &c. There were
about 20 queries difcuffed at *Swanfea*, all upon difcipline. We
have no names figning here.

1703. At *Llanwenarth*, the 18th of *May*, feveral queries
were propofed, and anfwers given; and it was agreed, that
no perfons except Meffengers only fhould attend confut-
tations and debates. Indeed, the primitive defign of affociating
was private confultation.

It was obferved, that, laft year, a fermon was appointed to
be preached this year, but we have no account by whom,
and poffibly no perfon was named ; but, at *Llanwenarth*, the
next affociation was appointed to be at *Swanfea*, and Brother
Richard Williams to preach. The whole was figned by the
Minifters above named in 1701, and, very probably, they
figned in 1702, though we have no account of it.

1704. The affociation met at *Swanfea* in the Whitfun-
week, 26th of *May*. There were fix or feven queries anfwered
here. This year's letter is not more than twenty lines.

It fays, that " the churches were moftly in peace and unity,
" enjoying an addition to their number; that the Minifters
" and Meffengers had a happy meeting, being all of one mind
" to follow what maketh for the peace and intereft of the
" churches; and that they, as one man, defire the churches
" to follow what maketh for their own peace, and not to let
" in fuch controverfial and difputable matters as may difturb
" their felicity."

It is figned by *Robert Morgan*, *John Jenkins*, *John Griffiths*, *Jofhua James*, *Richard Williams*, *Abel Morgan*, *Morgan
Griffiths*, *Morgan Jones*, *Thomas Price*, *William Phillips*, *Nathan Davis*, and *Caleb Evans*. There are nine more, feveral
of them in the miniftry, and fome Meffengers. Here they
defire every church to take care to keep up in practice the fix
principles mentioned in *Hebrews* vi. 1, 2.

The

The heroic and very venerable *Lewis Thomas* did not sign at this meeting. At his own place, in former years, his name was always the first; but, in the *March* preceding this meeting, he went to rest. He was the successor of the justly celebrated *John Myles* who fled from persecution to *America*, where he met with many trying exercises, but served the cause of Christ and his people very honourably. *Mr. Lewis Thomas* succeeded at *Ilston, Swansea*, &c. and stood his ground, was meek as a lamb, laborious as the ox, and bold as a lion. He not only served his own church through the persecution, but visited, comforted, and animated the other churches far and near. Aged people, about 40 years ago, spake very cordially in his praise. An elegy upon his death notes that many souls had been converted under his ministry; that, though he was plundered and imprisoned, he would not forsake his profession, and sin against God. His aged colleague, *Mr. R. Morgan*, was now feeble, so the proper successor to *Mr. L. Thomas* was *Mr. Morgan Jones*; his grandson, of the same name, lives now at *Hammersmith*, near *London*.

At the above meeting, it was desired, that the churches would take care to send one or two of the most fit and judicious brethren to the association as Messengers; and one or two of the most likely young brethren, that they also might learn for futurity.

They appointed the next meeting to be at *Llanwenarth*, and *Brother Philip James* to preach the association sermon. This gentleman was a native of the parish where *Mr. Robert Morgan* lived, and was educated for the establishment; but his embracing religion among the persecuted Baptists, procured him the frowns of his wealthy parents, so that he could not live comfortably in that country. He was pastor of the Baptist church at *Warwick* for a number of years, and from thence removed to the church at *Hampstead, Herts*, of which he was pastor many years. He had such knowledge and skill in physic that his common title was *Dr. James*. He died there in 1748, far advanced in years. The late worthy Rev. *Mr. Samuel James*, of *Hitchin*, in the same county, was his son.

This year, another branch of *Rhydwilim* church, which met at *Kilcam*, and *Kilvowyr*, formed into a church, and, for their pastor, they chose *Mr. Samuel Jones*, who was one of their number, and had long laboured among them with great acceptance. This made the *tenth* church.

1705. The association met at *Llanwenarth*, May 29. Here nine churches are named in tolerable order. The new church at *Kilcam* is called *Whitchurch*, the name of the parish; and *Glandwr* is called *Velindre*, the place, perhaps, where they then mostly met. *Trosgoed* is not named, but included in *Olchon*, as they had but one pastor. *Llantrisaint* was declining, and it seems sent no Messenger. The Letter this year was not much, if any, more than half as long as last year. Here three

queries

queries upon discipline are judiciously answered. Thirteen persons signed; *William Prichard* the first. They had all signed the last time but he and *Thomas Parry*. Here it is said; "Let every church take care to provide money according to their ability, to bear the expenses of their Ministers and Messengers to and from the association, and likewise to contribute, if there be occasion, to other necessities."

Next association to be at *Swansea*, to begin *Tuesday* in the Whitsun-week, *Brother Abel Morgan* to preach, or, otherwise, *Brother Morgan Griffiths*. This is the first time we notice any one named in case of failure.

About this time two worthy men died, who ought to be had in everlasting remembrance, especially among our denomination.

1st. Mr. *Griffith Howell,* who is supposed to have been the first baptized by *Mr. W. Jones* in *Pembrokeshire*. He was a gentleman of property, and lived at *Rushacre*, his own estate. His house was the first and chief place of worship among our friends for many years. He also was in the ministry; a remarkably hospitable man; generous in various ways. He wore well through all the persecution, and, after it, travelled far and near.

2d. Mr. *John Evans*, of *Llwyndwr*, near *Ynys-vach*. He was designed for the ministry in the establishment, and sent to grammar school with that view: but, when fit for *Oxford*, instead of going to the *University*, he joined the *Baptists*, and was baptized in 1673, when *Mr. Griffith Howell* was in prison for religion, according to the information of his worthy and aged daughter.

These three, *G. Howell*, *J. Evans*, and *Thomas David* were pillars to bear up this poor church in troublesome times; one lived near *Glandwr*, the other near *Ynys-vach*, and the third at *Rushacre*. Mrs. *Griffiths*, late of *Glanrhyd*, was Mr. *J. Evans*'s daughter, and furnished out many particulars respecting her father. She was a worthy member at *Rhydwilim* for many years. She died in 1776, aged 86. Her son, E. *Griffiths*, *Esq*. is in the commission of the peace, a gentleman of reputation, a judicious, active magistrate, attends at meeting, is very useful to the church, friendly, hospitable, and ready to assist.

1706. *Swansea*, *Whitsun-week*. The Messengers met according to appointment, but understood that there was a pressgang in the town, and, at that time, they were very eager to press young men, especially from among the Baptists. The ministers consulted and agreed, that it would be prudent to drop the public meeting, and disappoint hostile designs; so they did, and went all home. But they appointed the next meeting to be at *Llanwenarth*, and Br. *Morgan Griffiths* to preach. This affair is recorded in the *Blaenau* Book, and then it is there added, That but few things happened at the association worthy to be recorded from that time to 1711.

1707. At *Llanwenarth*, fourth of the fourth month. Three queries were answered. The letter is short, as before. It observes, that the churches were in peace, some much enlarged. The next meeting to be at *Rhydwillim*, in the *Whitsun-week*, Brother *Nathan Davis*, or Brother *Caleb Evans* to preach.

No names to our copy of this year. A fast to be kept in every church before the next association.

Mr. *Morgan Edwards's* materials, page 22, say, that Mr. *Owen Thomas* was a native of *Kilmaenllwyd* parish, went to *America* this year, 1707, and in 1740 became pastor of the church at *Welsh Tract*, mentioned above. Mr. *Thomas Griffiths* was the first pastor there, as already observed. He was succeeded by *Elisha Thomas*, who is supposed to have been a son of the very useful *Thomas David Rees*. The next successor there was Mr. *Enoch Morgan*, a younger brother to Mr. *Abel Morgan*, mentioned above. The former had a son named *Abel*, after the uncle. But nephew and son outshone the uncle and father in *America*, for many years. Mr. *Abel Morgan*, jun. is lately dead, but though dead, he will speak in that country for a long time to come. *Kilmaenllwyd* is not far from *Rhydwilim*; many of the members have lived in that parish; whether Mr. *Owen Thomas* was a son of any of them may now be uncertain. But it is remarkable, that three of the pastors of that church should fail on the same bottom, then succeed each other, and that the next successor should be from *Kilmaenllwyd*. And still, that the next pastor also of that church should be from the same country. He served with great repute to his death in 1769.

1708. *Rhydwilim*, 25 May. This is the first association *west* of *Carmarthen*. Hitherto we see, it had been kept in the *east*, alternately at *Llanwenarth* and *Swansea;* and it is supposed that affairs belonging to it were debated chiefly in *English*, as the writings relative to it are so. But after this year, their transactions were in *Welsh*; though some of the churches continued to write their letters in *English*. Henceforward the association met at different places. The letter of this year is longer than two or three former ones. It complains of lukewarmness, want of love and zeal. There had been consultations for some years at the associations, about assisting poor members: they did not approve of their going from one church to another, but thought it best for the churches to make collections among themselves, that particularly distressed cases might be relieved. This year, thanks were returned to the churches for their readiness to contribute. Three members, in each church, were appointed to take care of those collections and distributions. The next association to be at *Trosgoed*, Brother *John Jenkins* to preach, or Brother *Samuel*

Samuel Jones. Mr. Nathaniel Jenkins was among those who signed this year. He was a promising young man. Mr. Morgan Edwards, in a letter, dated 5th of November 1784, at Newark, Pennsylvania, says, "That Mr. Nathaniel Jenkins was a native of Cardiganshire, born 25th of March 1678, came to America an ordained minister in 1710, settled pastor of a new church at Cape-may, Jersey; in 1712, where he continued to 1730, then removed to Cohansy, where he continued to his death in 1754." During the 44 years he lived in that country, he acquitted himself with no small honour. While in his native country, he was in great repute. Aged people have been heard * to speak of him very respectfully. It seems he was originally a member of the Glandwr church.

1709. Trosgoed †, Whitsun-week. Of this meeting we have not been able to find any account; nor do we yet know where the next was. About this time were removed three other worthies, in some respects, though not in all, of more worth than the three mentioned in 1705, Messrs. *Thomas Quarrel, Robert Morgan* and *Thomas Parry*. We have said, that the former was pastor at *Shrewsbury*, in the time of the Commonwealth, about 1653, and he is named among the ejected ministers about 1660, before he settled at *Langwm*. He wore well to old age.

Mr. *Robert Morgan* signed at the three General Meetings in 1653 and 54, as a messenger from *Carmarthen*. It is not certain whether he was then in the ministry. When the *Carmarthen* church broke up in the troublesome times, he, with others, very probably, joined *Ilston* church, and was a colleague with Mr. *Lewis Thomas*, serving that church and *Craig-yr-allt*, as observed before. He kept a school great part of his days, and reared a large family through the many hardships of those times. He had a son whose name was *John*, a very promising young man for the ministry, of considerable literature. He was chosen by the church at *Warwick*; and accepted the invitation. He took leave of his friends cheerfully, but died in about a week, and was buried in the meeting-house in *Warwick*, with this inscription on his stone; " *To the memory of Mr. John Morgan, of Landilo, in Glamorganshire, Minister of the Gospel. He departed this life the 12th of May* 1703, *in the 24th year of his age.*

Sist' advena——Mors tibi etiam propinqua est."

He was the immediate predecessor of Dr. *James*, above named, who probably composed the inscription; they were both of the same parish. It is rather extraordinary, that Mr. *Reece*, the present pastor at *Warwick*, should be a native of the same parish. It is conjectured that Mr. *Robert Morgan*'s eldest son,

---

* By the Author of this History.
† The Rev. Author of this History was a member of the church at Trosgoed eight years. EDITOR.

of his own name, was the firſt ſchoolmaſter of the charity-ſchool, ſet up by the Diſſenters on *Horſley-Down, Southwark, London*; being then a member, and an occaſional teacher in Mr. *Stinton's* church, afterwards Dr. *Gill's*, now Mr. *Rippon's*. He behaved well in that place till his death in 1723. Mr. *R. Morgan*, ſen. it ſeems, was not a popular preacher, but an intelligent man. He correſponded with Mr. *Keach*; one or two of his letters are yet in being.

Mr. *Thomas Parry* ſigned at the meeting in *Abergavenny*, in 1653; he became ſerious about 1640; he was a plain country man, occupied a little farm, and ſometimes followed a trade; went not much from home, kept the meeting at his own houſe, was truly uſeful, and bore a very good character. Some of his great grandchildren, and their children, are now members among the baptiſts in *London*, one at *Leominſter*, and others in *Wales*.

1710. We have not found where the aſſociation was held this year. An article or two may be inſerted here.

1. From the beginning to this time *Craig-yr-allt* church met to worſhip at different friends houſes, as it ſuited; but the paſtor Mr. *M. Griffiths* obſerved, that when the Lord's ſupper was adminiſtered, none but the members would ſtop to ſee it. This year they erected a very good and decent meeting-houſe. It is in the pariſh of *Kelligar*, and called *Cefn-Hengoed*, pronounced *Keven Hengoed*, but, for brevity, commonly called *Hengoed*; and ſo we ſhall call it.——A few years before this, Mr. *David Rees* was raiſed up in this church, and became a worthy goſpel miniſter. At length he was choſen paſtor of the baptiſt church at *Limehouſe, London*. He diſcharged the duties of his ſtation with great repute, about forty years. He died in 1748. His funeral ſermon was preached by the late Dr. *Joſeph Stennett*, who had been long intimate with him. The ſermon is printed, and contains a good character of the deceaſed. In it, the Doctor, ſpeaking of his ordination, ſays, " The public work of that day fell chiefly on my honored Father, and the late *Rev. Mr. J. Piggott*."

2. Emigration. Mr. *Morgan Edwards's* Materials name three who arrived in *America* in 1710, Meſſrs. *Jenkin Jones, Benjamin Griffiths, and David Davis*. Though neither of them appears to have been a church member then, yet the three became miniſters of no ſmall repute in *America*, as is well known there. The former went from *Pembrokeſhire*, and was the firſt paſtor of the baptiſt church at * *Philadelphia*. He died in 1761. The ſecond was a half brother to Meſſrs. *Abel* and *Enoch Morgan*, by the ſame mother. He became intimate and connected with ſeveral baptiſts from the borders of the counties of *Radnor* and *Montgomery*, in *Wales*, according to which names they called parts of

* See a pleaſing account of him in Edwards's Materials towards a hiſtory of the Baptiſts in Pennſylvania, p. 41---46.

their new plantations. He was the first pastor of the church at *Montgomery*, in *Pennsylvania*. He had a colleague from *Radnorshire*, Mr. *Joseph Eaton*. Mr. *Benjamin Griffiths* was a long while pastor of that church, even to his death in 1768, aged 88. His son *Abel* is in the ministry now in that country, or was lately. Mr. *Edwards's* Materials inform us, that for the original of this church, " we must look back to 1710, when *John Evans* and wife, members of a baptist church in *Wales*, whereof *James James* was pastor; and next year *John James* and wife, members at *Rhydwilim*, arrived," &c. Very likely Mr. *B. Griffiths* went over with Mr. *John Evans*, being neighbours in their native country.——Mr. *D. Davis* was the fifth pastor at *Welsh Tract*, as hinted above, and died in 1769. These three worthies emigrated the same year, probably in the same vessel.

1711. The association was this year, it is supposed, at *Hengoed*, as they had now a convenient meeting-house, which they had not before. We have no account of the transactions here but what is hinted in the *Blaenau* book in 1706, recited above, that nothing material occurred in those meetings till 1711, this year perhaps included.

We have two emigrations this year. 1. Mr. *Abel Morgan*, the beloved pastor at *Blaenau*, in *Monmouthshire*. His brother *Enoch*, and many of his acquaintance, were gone ten years before. He also was a native of *Cardiganshire*, and other friends had failed the preceding year, as just now observed. A particular account is preserved of the very affectionate manner in which he parted from his friends, and of the rough weather, and great trials he had on the sea: his wife and child, a son, died in the voyage: he was twenty-two weeks from the time he went aboard to the time he landed. He sent back an affectionate moving letter, in *Welsh*, to his friends, giving a mournful, yet thankful detail of his voyage, and added, that he was soon to be at the ordination and settling of his dear brother *N. Jenkins*, with the new church in the *Jersey*. He soon took the leading care of the church at *Pennepec* and *Philadelphia*, though Mr. *Samuel Jones* was there, and had been above twenty years. They both lived in harmony, and died the same year; the latter in February 1722, and the former in December ensuing.

2. Mr. *Hugh Davis*. Mr. *Edwards's* Materials say that he was a native of *Cardiganshire*, baptized and ordained at *Rydwilim*, and arrived in *America* the 26th of April 1711. In the *Swanfey* records is the following account, which, very probably, Mr. *Edwards* had not seen. As there were so many emigrations from the Principality to *America*, possibly the Reader may not be displeased with a copy of a recommendatory letter, taken from the *Swansea* church book.

South Wales in *Great Britain.*

The church of Jesus Christ meeting at *Swansea* in *Glamorganshire*, owning believers baptism, laying on of hands, the doctrine of personal election, and final perseverance:

To any church of Jesus Christ, in the province of *Pennsylvania*, in *America*, of the same faith and order, whom this may concern.——Sendeth christian salutation: grace, mercy, and peace be multiplied unto you, from God the Father, through our Lord Jesus Christ. Amen.

Dearly beloved brethren in our Lord Jesus Christ,

Whereas our dearly beloved brethren and sisters, by name, *Hugh David (an ordained minister), and his wife Margaret, Anthony Matthew, Simon Matthew, Morgan Thomas, Samuel Hugh, Simon Butler, Arthur Melchior, and Hannah* his wife, design, by God's permission, to come with Brother *Sorency* to the aforesaid province of *Pennsylvania*; this is to testify unto you, that all the abovementioned are in full communion with us, and we commit all of them, to your christian care, beseeching you therefore to receive them in the Lord, watching over them, and performing all christian duties towards them as becometh saints to their fellow members. So we commit you, and them, to the Lord, and to the word of his grace, which is able to build you and them up on the most holy faith.

That the peace of God may sanctify you wholly, and that your and their spirits, souls, and bodies, may be preserved blameless unto the coming of our Lord Jesus Christ, shall be the earnest prayer of

Dated the 3d of the 7th month 1710; signed at our meeting by a part for the whole.

Your brethren in the faith and Fellowship of the gospel,
Morgan Jones,
John David,
William Matthews,
and 11 more.

These nine, it is probable, were from some parts of *Swansea* church, except the minister and his wife, who also were now in full communion with them, having been dismissed from *Rhydwilim*.

Of Mr. *Simon Butler* much might be said; suffice it here to observe, that he turned out a great and worthy man; his common title, long before he died, was *Esquire Butler*. He died in 1764, aged 77. *Hannah Melchior* was a daughter of Mr. *Robert Morgan* abovementioned.

The *Materials* so often referred to, inform us, that the church of *Great Valley*, in *Pennsylvania*, originated from several persons, with their families, that arrived from *Wales* in 1701 and 1702, of which one was *James Davis*, a member from *Rhydwilim*, and another was *Richard Myles*, who had been a hearer of Mr. *Henry Gregory*, in *Radnorshire*, but who was baptized in *America*. By the religious industry of these two families, who obtained ministers to preach at their houses, some were baptized. The lot of Mr, *Hugh Davis* (called *David* in the above letter), and some others, happened to fall near them, which increased their number to sixteen. They formed themselves into a church in 1711, and chose Mr. *Hugh Davis* their pastor. He served them till he died in 1753. This was the third Baptist church in *Pennsylvania*.

1712. *Llanwenarth*, June. We have not the letter of this year, nor any information who preached. But this query was proposed, Whether there were to be ruling elders in the church? The answer was given in the affirmative. The *Materials* inform us, that Mr. *W. Thomas*, born in *Llanwenarth*, arrived in *America* 14th of *February* 1712; was many years an assistant in the ministry to Mr. *B. Griffiths*, at *Montgomery*, died in 1757, and that his son, Mr. *John Thomas*, was his assistant and succeeded in the pastoral care of that church. Mr. *William Thomas* was a member at *Blaenau*, lived at a place called *Rhassau*, where a branch of the church met. It is thought, that he emigrated along with the pastor, though the *Materials* mention a year to a day between their arrivals. Mr. *Abel Morgan* went aboard the vessel at *Bristol*, on Sept. 11, and was twenty-two weeks before he quitted the ship; so he arrived in Feb. 1711-12, according to the way of dating before the style was altered in 1752. Mr. *A. Morgan* might date, in the way of the last century, when the year ended with February. The letter, giving an account of the voyage, is dated April 1712. In it he desires the *Blaenau* church to take care of the meeting at *Rhassau*.

1713. *Rhydwilim*, 26th and 27th of May. The Circular Letter fills two pages folio, closely written. It is a solid, sensible epistle. It laments declining religion in some places; the removal, by death, "of *so many* of the most eminent ones in "grace and holiness;" and the numbers gone to *America*. No account who preached. The method then was only to name who was appointed for the following year. Next association to be at *Swansea*, in the Whitsun-week, Brother *Nathan Davis* to preach. A day of fasting and prayer to be observed the first of July, and another to be in the week before the next association. The leading ministers now were Messrs. *John Jenkins, Richard Williams, Nathan Davis* and *Morgan Griffiths*: others who signed here, were *Caleb Evans, John Harris, Timothy Lewis, Samuel Jones, Thomas Matthias* and *James Williams*.

Mr. *Edwards* observes, that in 1713, Mr. *John Davis*, from *Pembrokeshire*, arrived in *America* ; was called to the ministry in 1722, and ordained in 1732; took part of the ministry with *H. Davis* at *Great Valley*, succeeded him there, and was alive in 1770, when the Materials were printed. He died in 1778. His funeral sermon was preached by Mr. (now Dr.) *S. Jones* of *Lower Dublin, Pennsylvania.* The famous Mr. *Enoch Francis* had now been a few years in the ministry ; he began at 19, and was a very promising acceptable young man. Several of his very dear friends, who had lately crossed the Atlantic, wrote to him

him, and warmly invited him to follow them; but he stuck close to his native country, and was eminently useful in it.

1714. *Swansea*, Whitsun-week. For want of the letter of this year, all we know is, that two Queries were answered here. It was now a very gloomy time in England; the Pretender was like to come in, and the Nonconformists were in great danger of another persecution; but on the 1st of August, ensuing this association, *Queen Anne* died, and was succeeded by *George* the First. This remarkable providence dispelled the gloom, and public thanksgivings, many years, were annually given by the Baptists in Wales for the deliverance of the 1st of August 1714.

1715. The *Blaenau* records say, that in 1715 no query was proposed. The association this year was at *Hengoed*; but not having the letter, we cannot say who preached. This year the meeting-house at *Blaenau* was built. Mr. *Abel Morgan* was succeeded there by Mr. *William Philips* and Mr. *John Harris*, both of whom were raised up in that church; the former was the senior man, but the latter the most able minister; he was very active at home and in assisting neighbouring churches. He collected the early account of the associations before and after 1700.

1716. *Llanwenarth*, May 22d and 23d. The letter of this year contains this paragraph, "We beseech you, that you continue and persevere in the way of truth, and never forget the late miraculous deliverance which the Lord wrought for us in this nation; when our enemies thought to make a prey of us, then did the Lord wonderfully deliver." This refers to the Rebellion in 1715, when several meeting-houses were pulled down in *England*, and two at *Wrexham*. The death of the Queen, on the 1st of August 1714, was considered as the beginning of the deliverance; therefore, at the close of the letter, they say, "We desire that you observe the 1st of August, and the first Wednesday of every month throughout the year, in rememberance of our late deliverance." Two queries were answered. Next association to be at *Blaenau*, in the Whitsun-week. Brother *John Jenkins* to preach; in case of failure, Brother *Nathan Davis*.

1717. *Blaenau*, June 12. The letter of this year is not long, but takes affectionate notice of the late deliverance, and the new favourable King; reminds the churches to observe the 1st of August, and the Wednesdays as before. Next association to be at *Llanelli*, Brother *Morgan Griffiths* to preach, in case of failure, Brother *John Harris*. The letter was signed by *Nathan Davis*, *Richard Williams*, *Morgan Griffiths*, *John Harris*, *Samuel Jones*, *Timothy Lewis*, *David James*, *Enoch Francis*, and *Thomas David*.

Radnorshire and *Llanafan* have been mentioned before more than once; they had now been long the same church, but had two ministers. Formerly Mr. *Thomas Evans* was in *Brecknockshire*, and the meeting was kept at his house, called *Pentre*. His
son,

son, Mr. *Caleb Evans*, succeeded in the *Pentre* part in *Brecknocshire.* In *Radnorshire*, formerly Mr. *Henry Gregory* was minister, but now Mr. *Nathan Davis*; their meeting place was called *Cwm*, commonly written in English *Coomb*. They had another meeting place in *Montgomeryshire*, called *Garth*, all one church. This year a mere trifle raised a sad contention among them, so that the *Pentre* part separated and administered ordinances among themselves. This affair was laid before the association, and grieved them much; they were sorry the *Pentre* part had gone so far; they considered the subject, disapproved the separation, gave their sentiments, and desired all the churches to keep the 25th of the same month to fast and pray on account of that church, that peace might be restored, and Satan rebuked, &c. This letter was signed by *Richard Williams, Philip Jones, Morgan Griffiths, John Harris, Morgan Jones, David James, Samuel Jones, James Williams,* and *Nicholas Edwards.*

January preceding this association, died the excellent Mr. *Timothy Thomas,* of *Pershore*, in *Worcestershire*, who had been a noted preacher in the counties of *Montgomery, Denbigh,* and *Flint,* before he removed to *Pershore* in 1696, though he was then only about twenty years of age.—A worthy man!

1718, *Llanelli,* Whitsun-week. *Llanelli* was a branch of *Swansea* church, but in *Carmarthenshire.* This letter takes particular notice of the indulgence of providence in placing such a King upon the throne.

1719. *Rhydwilim,* Whitsunweek. The letter this year consisted of warnings and cautions to the churches. They were reminded of the above-mentioned days of prayer, and were exhorted to beware of sin, contention, &c. The reconciliation was not yet made between *Coomb* and *Pentre.* Queries were answered. The next association to be at *Trosgoed*; Brother *John Jenkins* to preach, if he fails, Brother *John Harris.* Several signed this letter.

On the 22d of February, preceding this meeting, the author of this History was born. About this time his father, and some neighbours, were strongly inclined to go to *America*: laying hold of the infant hand of his new-born child, he said, " This little hand, probably, will hereafter be ridding and clearing land in *Pennsylvania."* But it was prevented, and Providence said, No.

1720. *Trosgoed,* Whitsun-week. This letter notes, that, in general, the churches were in peace, and great additions were made to some. Direction was given how to behave towards young men beginning to preach. particularly not to encourage the bold and forward; nor to discourage the low and diffident in their own eyes. About that time, there were two young men, in different churches, of whom Mr. *David Rees*'s father said, " The people cannot keep R. W. out of the pulpit, nor put E. E. in." The former caused great trouble, and turned out erroneous in doctrine, and profane in practice. The other wore very well to old age, but never would be ordained; yet was an excellent affiftant in the miniftry during life and ftrength. Here it was ordered that the circular letter fhould be read twice in the year, and days of thankfgiving were agreed upon, as before. The next affociation to be at *Coomb, Radnorfhire*, in the Whitfun-week, Brother *John Harris* to preach, or Brother *Enoch Francis*. Signed by *John Jenkins, Jofhua James, Morgan Griffiths, John Harris, William Philips, Thomas Price, Richard Williams*, and feven more, who probably were not minifters.

Mr. *Philip Jones* died about this time. He was among thofe who figned the refult of the confultation upon the affair at *Coomb* and *Pentre* in 1717. He was an affifting minifter at *Rhydwilim*. From feveral circumftances it is conjectured, that his brother removed to live in *Gloucefterfhire*, and was father to the late venerable Mr. *Philip Jones*, paftor of the church at *Upton* upon *Severn*; which he ferved with deferved repute about forty years; and his fon, Mr. *Edmund Jones*, was a very refpectable minifter and paftor of the baptift church at *Exon, Devon*, where he died 15th of April 1765, aged 43.

1721. *Coomb*, 30th, and 31ft of May. This letter notes in the general, the peace and profperity of the churches; and mingles various complaints of negligence and lukewarmnefs, with fuitable exhortations and motives. Two queries were anfwered well. Days of thankfgiving ftill continued. The next affociation to be at *Hengoed*, Brother *Enoch Francis* to preach, or Brother *William Meredith*, who was a worthy helper at *Llanwenarth* for many years. Signed by *John Harris, Enoch Francis, Nathan Davis, William Davis, M. Griffiths, David James, Richard Williams, Morgan Jones, William Meredith, Timothy Lewis*, &c.

Though the letter fays nothing of the reftoration of peace between *Coomb* and *Pentre*, yet this meeting promoted it, and foon after it was brought about. The terms of the reconciliation are inferted in the *Blaenau* church book by Mr. *John Harris*, who was a valuable recorder. This year the Baptift Confeffion of Faith, fet forth in *London* 1689, was publifhed in *Welfh*. Some churches had, before this, wrote Confeffions themfelves, but agreeable to that form of found words.

In 1721, Mr. *Jofeph Price* died, aged 60. He was a native of the *Hay* parifh, in *Brecknockfhire*, and preached at *Llanigon, Pentre*, &c. before 1689. He undertook the paftoral care at *Tewkfbury*, in *Gloucefterfhire*, 1695, where he was very acceptable and ufeful, as well as in the neighbouring churches, till he finifhed his courfe.

1722. *Hengoed*, 15th and 16th of May. Caufes of joy and forrow are mentioned in this letter, and emphatical obfervations made on the great deliverance by the acceffion of King *George*, with a charge given to mind the days of thankfgiving. By this letter, it appears, that contention had begun in a church not named; healing meafures were propofed. Next affociation to be be at *Llanwenarth*, Brother *David James* to preach, or Brother *Nathan Davis*. This year the indefatigable *Abel Morgan* rested from his labours in *Pennsylvania*, having served his generation in that country near ten years. He had a particular hand in raising the church at *Montgomery*, in that province, with spiritual materials from the Ancient Britons. He helped to form them into a church in 1719; and the very year he died, this young church, very probably by his direction, called to the ministry Messrs. *Benjamin Griffiths* and *Joseph Eaton*, both from *Wales*, as noted above, and soon after they were both ordained, as appears from Mr. *M. Edwards*'s materials. Mr. *A. Morgan* was but about 49 when he died. *Montgomery* was the fifth baptist church in *Pennsylvania*, of which four originated from the Principality.

The worthy assistant to Dr. *Price*, about 1689, Mr. *Nathaniel Morgan*, named above, died 21st of November 1722, aged 71. He lived the latter part of his time at *Usk Castle*, *Monmouthshire*. Besides the present Dr. *S. Stennett's* mother, he had several amiable daughters, married into religious and respectable families in *England*; it is said, one to Mr. *Roberts* of *Abingdon*, another to Mr. *Noble* of *Bridgewater*, &c.

1723. *Llanwenarth*, Whitsun-week. The letter of this year mentions additions to most of the churches. Mr. *John Harris* was now translating into *Welsh*, a book, intitled, " New Heavens and a new Earth;" and he was here encouraged to proceed. A query was answered. Thanksgiving days still recommended. Hint of the contention mentioned last year, but no church named. The next association to be at *Blaenau*, Brother *Nathan Davis* to preach, in case of failure Brother *Samuel Jones*. Signed by *Richard Williams*, *John Jenkins*, *Joshua James*, *John Harris*, *Morgan Griffiths*, *William Meredith*, *John Evans*, *Roger Walker*, *Philip Morgan*, *John Philips*, &c. Mr. *John Evans* was a brother and assistant to Mr. *Caleb Evans*, at *Pentre*; Mr. *Roger Walker*, a son-in-law and assistant to Mr. *N. Davis* at *Coomb*; Mr. *Philip Morgan*, a young assistant at *Trofgoed*, and Mr. *John Philips*, a young candidate at *Rhydwilim*.

1724. *Blaenau*, Whitsun-week. Many added to some of the churches. But this was a most afflictive meeting; the contention mentioned the two preceding years was by this time grown to an awful height, from a mere trifle, and it was in the famous and excellent church at *Rhydwilim*. They were now split into two parties, each administering ordinances, receiving members, &c. one party consisting of about eighty members, and the other of about one hundred and forty. Mr. *John Jenkins* with one part, and Mr. *David James* with the other. The ministers here were grieved much on account of it; Mr. *Joshua James*, the pastor at *Llanwenarth*, did all he could to reconcile matters, and others assisted, but all failed him.

In the letter, there are affectionate exhortations and motives to love, peace, and self-denial. The first Wednesday of each month

month, for half a year, was appointed for fasting and prayer, on account of this distressing affair. Next association to be at the new meeting-house near *Llanelli*, a branch of *Swansea* church. Brother *Samuel Jones* to preach, or Brother *William Meredith*. The churches were requested to pray earnestly that the next meeting might be more comfortable. The letter was signed by twenty ministers and messengers. The aged and respectable Mr. *Richard Williams* was not among them; he died this year, perhaps before the meeting. He had faithfully served *Trosgoed*, *Olchon*, and *Llanigon*, for many years; he was a remarkable peace-maker. They had a plenty of trouble after he was gone to rest.

1725. *Llanelli*, 18th and 19th of May. A mournful letter. The appearance of the churches not as in years past: from the beginning they commonly commended the churches for their readiness to send their messengers to their association; but now they complain that messengers were not sent, who might be very useful in the meeting. Indeed, ministers and messengers were much grieved the preceding year: yet, after all, this meeting ended comfortably: the two ministers at the head of the parties at *Rhydwilim* were present, and each acknowledged his fault, and a foundation was laid for a happy reconciliation. This was in answer to many fervent prayers in public and in private. At this meeting there was a query received from *Llantrisaint*; that church was rather in a dying state. The churches were desired to observe days of thanksgiving for what was done towards peace, in proportion to their days of prayer last year. The next meeting to be at *Cilfowyr*, (pronounced *Kilvowyr*) formerly *Cilcam*. Brother *Caleb Evans* to preach, or Brother *William Philips*; the latter was the senior minister at *Blaenau*. Signed by *Nathan Davis*, *Morgan Jones*, *Samuel Jones*, *William Phillips*, *James Williams*, *Caleb Evans*, *Abel Francis*, *Griffith Jones*, *Evan Edward*, *Miles Harris*, and six more.

1726. *Cilfowyr*, Whitsun-week. The meeting-house here was built ten years before. It is rather a wonder the association had not met in it sooner. This letter observes, that the churches were mostly at peace, but laments much the bad effects of contention and strife. The *Rhydwilim* affair was here finished, and directions were given to cultivate and establish peace. Mr. *David James* died before this meeting, but he was at the last, and so at the beginning of the peace. There were valuable men on each side in this unhappy contention. But through the goodness of God it ended well; it is recorded here as a caution to future ages. There were two queries from *Llantrisaint*. The brethren about *Pontypool*, in *Monmouthshire*, wished to build a meeting-house, and to be assisted. The next association to be at *Swansea*; Brother *Nathan Davis* to preach, or Brother *Morgan Griffiths*. Signed by *N. Davis*, *Morgan Griffiths*, *John Harris*, *Samuel Jones*, *William Meredith*, *Caleb Evans*, *Enoch Francis*, *John Jenkins*, *Thomas Matthias*, *Miles Harris*, *Griffith Jones*, &c. Soon after this meeting *Nathan Davis* finished his course, for he

died

died the 8th of June 1726, aged 63. It is rather fingular
that three fucceffive paftors fhould each die at the age of 63, yet
fo it happened here to Meffrs. *Henry Gregory*, *N. Davis*, and
Roger Walker; likewife Mr. *Caleb Evans*, a colleague with Mr.
N. Davis, and Mr. *John Harris* of *Blaenau*, died at the fame
age. It is eafy to learn how acceptable Mr. *N. Davis* was
in his miniftry, from his being fo often appointed to preach at
the affociation. He was warm and manly in his natural temper
quick and ready in his minifterial talents.

Here it may be noted, that *Llantrifaint* has been mentioned
in the number of churches from the beginning; though it was
very low after the death of Mr. *Quarrel*: it was called alfo
Llangwm, *Ufk*, &c. It bore the laft name, efpecially while
Mr. *N. Morgan* lived there, and preached at the Caftle, or near
it. After his death there was a kind of a new formation of it
at *Lantrifaint* again; but ftill it was weak.

Till this time we have had no account of any new church
fince 1704, but this year *Pen-y-vai* was conftituted; the conftituents were members of *Swanfea* and *Hengoed*. They chofe Mr.
Griffith Jones, abovenamed more than once, for their paftor. He
was fon of Mr. *Morgan Jones*, the paftor of *Swanfea*. Now
the churches were 12 in number.

1727. *Swanfea*, 23d and 24th of May. Here the brethren ex-
prefs their joy that the meeting was more comfortable than in
years paft, and that peace was reftored; and that in fome places
a wide door was opened to preach the gofpel. Here was fome
debate about the eternal filiation or generation of the Son of God:
but it was advifed, that minifters fhould preach the plain, clear
gofpel, and not puzzle the people with inexplicable myfteries.
Here was fome debate alfo about preaching to finners; and
feveral reafons were given for it. The next meeting to be at
Rhydwilim, Brother *Morgan Jones* to preach, or Brother *Enoch
Francis*.

The perfons who began the above debates were confidered as
fwerving from the truth, therefore the churches were defired to
keep a day of fafting and prayer on their account, the laft week
in June; and they were advifed to be peculiarly cautious in the
calling of young men to the miniftry. Signed by *Morgan
Griffiths*, *Morgan Jones*, *John Harris*, *Enoch Francis*, *Caleb
Evans*, *John Davis*, *Roger David*, *Samuel Jones*, &c.

There were terms in the reconciliation between *Pentre* and
Coomb, that were to continue during the lives of the two minifters, in their alternate way of preaching, &c. When Mr. *N.
Davis* died, thefe terms were no longer binding, and the two
focieties feparated. Then *Pentre* fent a letter to the affociation,
and has been ever fince a feparate church. This made the number 13.

1728. *Rhydwilim*, 11th and 12th of June. This is a very good
and affectionate letter. It contains comfortable accounts from the
churches, all in peace, and moft of them profperous. One
church

church wished to have fixed days for preaching on church order, discipline, duties of members, &c. It does not appear whether this was agreed to. But it is observed, that the ministers who agitated the debates of last year, agreed with the association for preaching to sinners. There were three young ministers about that time who joined in some singularities. But it is supposed that it was the man mentioned above, *who could not be kept out of the pulpit* *, that led the other two. He was silenced long before he died. The other two resigned the ministry. The writer of these pages long knew the three, and hopes well of two of them; one of them was, he believes, very orthodox; the other had his peculiarities about the person of Christ, but was a serious man, and inoffensive in his morals.

The churches are directed to read the letter of 1720. The next association to be at *Llangloffan* Brother *Enoch Francis* to preach, or in case of failure, Brother *John Philips*. Mr. *Joshua James*, pastor at *Llanwenarth*, died in 1728; a worthy minister.

1729. *Llangloffan*, Whitsun-week. This place was a distant, but fruitful branch of *Rhydwilim*. Complaints were now made of some churches who only sent their letters, but no messengers, to the association. The catechism, perhaps that by Mr. *Keach*, and *Cole* on God's Sovereignty, to be both reprinted in Welsh. Arminian doctrines now gave uneasiness to the Baptists. They had made disturbances among the Independents and Presbyterians, for near twenty years before, soon after the disputes in *London* about Dr. *Crisp*'s works, and Dr. *Daniel Williams*'s writings. The latter was a native of *Wrexham*.

The sermon preached here by Mr. *E. Francis*, upon Cant. viii. 12. was printed. It does not appear that any of the association sermons had been printed before, or for a long while after. The next association to be at *Hengoed*, brother *John Jenkins* to preach, or Brother *Caleb Evans*. Many signed as usual; *David Owen* from *Llanelli*, and *Thomas Jones* of *Penyvai*, for the first time.

The meeting-house near *Pontypool*, mentioned in 1727, was this year finished, and a new church was formed. The constituents were members from *Blaenau*, *Llanwenarth*, and *Hengoed*, who were situated conveniently. Their first pastor was Mr. *Miles Harris*, then a very popular preacher, and of great acceptance. Now they were 14 churches.

1730. *Hengoed*. As the letter of this year never came to our hands, we can give no epitome of it; but the meeting was uncomfortable. There were very warm debates upon general redemption, and other articles connected with it. Mr. *E. Francis*, it has been said, had work enough to moderate some tempers. His own disposition was excellent, and he was a man of no small influence. Mr. *Charles Winter*, a member at *Hengoed*, was promising for the ministry, and was encouraged to

---

* See page 39, of this History.

go to *Briftol* for further improvement under Mr. *Fofkett's* care, but he chofe to go to *Carmarthen*, under Mr. *Perrot*, whofe fcholars and pupils were of the Remonftrants fide, at leaft feveral of them. Mr. *Winter*, and one or two more of the *Hengoed* members, at this meeting, pleaded for thofe doctrines againft the minifters. There were about thirty of that church who fided with Mr. *Winter*, and there was a talk then of a feparation. Mr. *David Rees*, from *London*, coming into the country to fee his friends, he interpofed, and things were quieted. By the intereft he had in the affections of both parties, they agreed to continue in communion; fo the debate ended then, but different opinions were ftill held. Mr. *Winter* continued to preach, but not openly, his peculiar tenets. He was of a quiet and peaceable temper. Mr. *Morgan Jones*, the worthy paftor of *Swanfea*, died in 1730. He was a valuable minifter, and had ferved in the church 40 years, or more.

1731. *Llanwenarth*, 8th and 9th of the 4th month. The doctrine of the Trinity, and other articles called Calviniftic, are fet in the preamble of this letter, which we never faw before in thofe letters. The churches are faid to be in peace; feveral added to many of them; difcipline obferved, and the unfound in doctrine excluded. It is noted further, how happy the ancient Britons were till the errors of Pelagius and Arminius came in like a flood. Minifters and people are exhorted to take heed to the truth. It is a good doctrinal and practical letter. It was a peaceable meeting. Not having the laft years letter, we know not who was appointed to preach here. As yet they did not mention in the letter who had preached at the affociation. Next meeting to be at *Blaenau*, Brother *Griffith Jones* to preach, or Brother *John Jenkins*. Several figned here, among them *Roger David*, the fucceeding paftor at *Llanwenarth*, and *David Owen* belonging to the *Llanelli* part of *Swanfea*.

In 1731, a new church was formed at *Molefton*, in *Pembrokefhire*. It had been another diftant branch of *Rhydwilim*. This was the third daughter of that mother church. The churches were now 15 in all.

1732. *Blaenau*, 30th and 31ft of May. The Confeffion of Faith was prefixed to this letter, like the laft. Joy was expreffed becaufe the churches did ftrive together againft errors, excluding thofe who extended redemption beyond election, &c. There was a query, " Whether it were neceffary and profitable to preach the reign of Chrift upon the earth 1000 years?" Reply. " That the Affociation in general looked upon that to be a truth, and under a bleffing, it might be profitable, when done with good light and underftanding, with much caution."

About 1726 or 1727, many had been added to *Blaenau* and *Hengoed*. This occafioned many debates about Baptifm. There were two young minifters then very zealous in the debate, Mr. *Miles Harris* for Believer's Baptifm, and Mr. *Edmund Jones* for
Infant

Infant Baptifm. It had at length fo difturbed the country, that both fides appointed a meeting upon the fubject; not fo much to debate it, as to take more care of tempers, cenfures, &c. There were feveral minifters prefent; fome conceffions made, and one forgave the other, and agreed in future to aim at the glory of God, the credit of the Gofpel, and the preferving of each other's reputation. The agreement was written, figned, attefted, and printed, on half a fheet. The Baptifts who figned were, Mr. *Griffiths*, of *Hengoed*, and Mr. *John Harris*, and Mr. *Miles Harris*, of *Blaenau;* the Pædopaptifts, Meffrs. *David Williams*, *Daniel Rogers*, and *Edmund Jones*, of *Pennymain; James Davis*, *Evan Joon*, and *Jenkin Lewis*, of *Merthyr-tydfil*; thefe were all paftors, preachers, or candidates. Five attefted the agreement; the firft of whom was Mr. *Fowler Walker*, the Independent minifter at *Abergavenny*. This agreement was attended to for fome years. It was dated in 1728. But early in 1732, a piece upon Infant Baptifm was publifhed in Englifh by Mr. *Walker*, the firft witnefs above. It was foon publifhed alfo in Welfh. For this reafon our brethren agreed, at the *Blaenau* affociation, to publifh, in Welfh, Mr. *Charles Doe*'s fmall tract of 40 texts of fcripture, on Believers Baptifm; and a letter was fent to Mr. *Walker*, by Mr. *David Rees*, of London, turned into Welfh, and printed the fame year, with a promife therein, that his book would be further confidered at leifure.

The next affociation to be at *Pen-y-fai*. Brother *John Jenkins* to preach, or Brother *Miles Harris*.

1733. *Pen-y-fai*, 15th and 16th of May. Here the churches are all named in the preamble, thus, *Pen-y-fai*, *Hengoed*, *Pen-y-garn*, *Llanwenarth*, *Blaenau*, *Llantrifaint*, *Llanigon*, *Swanfea, Cilfowyr*, *Rhyd-wilim*, *Pentre*, *Rock*, *Molefton*, and *Newcaftle*. Thefe muft be a little explained, to make out the *fifteen*. Here are but fourteen names. *Olchon* and *Trofgoed* were two before Mr. *Richard Williams* came to them; during his time they were as one; after his death, they were for years uncomfortable, and unfettled; but, in 1729, they feparated again, and *Llanigon* then joined *Trofgoed*. In 1731, Mr. *Philip Morgan* was fettled and ordained at the place laft mentioned, and Mr. *W. Williams*, a young man from *Cilfowyr*, fettled at *Olchon*, the fame year. It feems, there was no meffenger from this place at *Pen-y-fai*, unlefs it is omitted in our copy. *Coomb* was now removed to *Rock*, and *Glandwr* to *Newcaftle*. By thefe new names they went for many years. So explained, the churches appear to be 15.

The letter complains of falfe doctrines publicly heard in the miniftry: with thefe two of the churches were affected for years: *Hengoed* is already mentioned; to which muft be added, *Newcaftle*, which was Mr. *E. Francis*'s own church. He publifhed a book on the fubject, in his mild and affectionate way, under this title, "A Word in Seafon." But his coufin Mr. *Abel Francis*

took

took the other fide, and preached his fentiments more openly than Mr. *Winter*, and about 1736, went gradually off to thofe Pædobaptifts, who were with him for general redemption.

Here it fhould be mentioned, that the venerable, worthy, and unwearied Mr. *John Jenkins* died 3d of July 1733, aged 77. This was foon after his long journey to *Pen-y-fai* that year, where he was appointed to preach: he was fucceeded by Mr. *Thomas Matthias*, who had long been his affiftant and colleague.

The next meeting to be at *Pen-y-garn*; Brother *E. Francis* to preach, or Brother *Roger David*. There were feventeen names to this letter, few of the old ones, Mr. *John Jenkins* is the firft, and this was his laft time of figning. The young ones were *Roger David, Thomas Williams, David Owen, John Morgan, Morgan Harris, John Davis, Thomas Jones, Wm. Davis,* &c. moft of whom are named above.

1734, *Pen-y-garn*, 5th June. This was the new church and new houfe near *Pontypool;* and THIS IS A KIND OF A NEW ÆRA TO THE ASSOCIATION. In imitation of the Weftern Convention, ours agreed to have an Affociation book, to write in it the circular letter annually, and for that purpofe it was to be carried to the yearly meeting. In the front of their letter they were defired to mention to the affociation, their agreement with the articles fet forth by the Elders and Brethren in London, in the year 1689. The churches were defired to confider things, and give their opinion next year. The letter, in future, was to mention who preached at the meeting, as well as who were appointed for the next meeting. It fays this year, That Brother *E. Francis* preached in Welfh, from Matt. xxiv. 45, and as an additional new favour, Brother *Fofkett* of *Briftol*, preached in Englifh, from 2 Tim. iv. 7. The letter expreffes joy that difagreeable debates were in a good meafure ceafed. The churches were informed that Mr. *D. Rees*'s Treatife on Baptifm, in anfwer to Mr. *Walker*, was out. It is a large and learned piece. The new church at *Molefton* had loft all their three officers in one year; their paftor Mr. *Griffith Williams*, a ruling Elder, and a Deacon; breaches indeed! The next meeting to be at *Llanelli*, Brother *Roger David* to preach, or Brother *Miles Harris*.— Fourteen figned.

In 1734, died the very aged paftor of *Glandwr*, then *Newcaftle* church, Mr. *James James*. He had been in a confiderable part of the perfecution. It is fuppofed he was fome years above eighty. Mr. *Francis* had now been a confiderable time the acting paftor of the church.

1735, *Llanelli*, Whitfun-week. An affectionate letter this year; the churches moftly in peace, and all of them named right in the front of the letter, except *Llanigon* put for *Trofgoed*. The agreement with the confeffion of 1689 is mentioned, and it continued to be fo, in the letters to and from the Affociation, generally, if not conftantly, till of late years. Here it was defired

fired that the letters from the churches might not be too long;
and after confultation, it was agreed, that *Llanelli* fhould be
formed into a church, and be no longer a branch of *Swanfea*. It
lay far on the Weft, and in *Carmarthenfhire*. Mr. *David Owen*,
one of themfelves, was ordained, and had been in the miniftry
about ten years. He was chofen to be their paftor, but as
Swanfea was yet unfettled, he was to affift there at times, by
agreement. Now there were 16 churches.

A fuitable and acceptable fermon was preached by Brother
Roger David, from 1 Tim. iv. 16. This letter was figned by
the former names, with the addition of *Evan Thomas*, the young
and worthy paftor at *Molefton*.

1736. *Rhydwilim*, 15th and 16th of June. Brother *Miles
Harris* preached, from Rom. x. 15, and in the evening Brother
Hugh Evans, of *Briftol*, from Ephefians iii. 8. He was fon of
Mr. *Caleb Evans*, of *Pentre*, and was then affiftant to Mr. *Fofkett*, at *Broadmead, Briftol.* There was here a query from
Trofgoed, "Whether perfons of different fentiments [*about laying
on of hands*] might be admitted to, and continued in, communion?"
The anfwer in the affirmative, provided they did not hold any
doctrines contrary to the word. The venerable, laborious, and
acceptable Mr. *Samuel Jones*, the firft paftor at *Cilfowyr*, finifhed
his courfe this year, aged 80. He was remarkable for his witti-
cifms, but ufed them to good purpofe. His fayings were long
remembered in the churches in *South Wales*, which he now and
then vifited.

1737. *Newcaftle*, Whitfun-week. This church was now of
full 40 years ftanding, yet never had the Affociation before.—
Probably it was for want of a convenient place. The letter
mentions peace in the churches, and an addition to all, except
one or two. Means of grace plenty, and hearers numerous. Brother *Morgan Griffiths* preached, from Acts xxvi. 28.

Hitherto the churches in Wales had been very ftrict for laying
on of hands on the baptized, ever fince 1689, or foon after.
Meffrs. *B. Keach* and *Wm. Rider* had been in this practice; but
there had been little debate about it till now. At *Trofgoed*, a
young man propofed for communion. Queftions being afked,
about laying on of hands, he acknowledged that he was not
clear in it. This caufed the fubject to be inveftigated. The
confequence was, that Mr. *Philip Morgan*, the paftor, and Mr.
Wm. Herbert, his colleague, were fully perfuaded that it was
not properly a gofpel ordinance. So upon this article there was
no fmall debate and warmth at *Newcaftle*. But the two minifters continued in their perfuafion during life, and it has been
feldom ufed in that church fince that time.

This year Mr. *Thomas Jones* of *Pen-y-fai*, and family, and
Mr. *Wm. Davis*, formerly at *Llantrifaint*, failed to *America*.
The former fettled in 1738, with a new church at *Tulpehokon*, in
Pennfylvania, and was ordained there in 1740. Moft, or all the
conftituents of this church, as well as their paftor, were from the

Principality

Principality. Mr. *Jones* continued in that place many years, and maintained an honourable character to the laft; but advancing in age, refigned the miniftry there, and preached occafionally. He died comfortably in 1788, in the 87th year of his age. A pleafing account of the circumftances of his death I had from his fon, the prefent juftly refpected Dr. *Samuel Jones,* paftor of the church at *Lower Dublin,* near *Philadelphia,* who was about three years of age when he failed with his father from *Pen-y-fai*; the letter is dated March 31, 1788, and runs thus, " The other day I attended the funeral of my honoured father. I paid him two or three vifits during his laft illnefs, and found him remarkably comfortable in his mind; his faith being ftrong, his hope firm, his evidences clear, his views of glory tranfporting, and his defires ardent; yet calm and refigned. Some of his laft words, when indeed he was fcarce able to fpeak, were, Joy! joy! joy!—The following is what appeared in our public prints on the occafion. " On Monday the 24th of March, departed this lif: ; in *Chefter* county, the Rev. *Thomas Jones,* in the 87th year of his age. The Thurfday following his remains were interred in the Baptift burial ground at *Tredyffryn,* attended by a large and refpectable concourfe of people; on which occafion a pathetic difcourfe was delivered from Matt. xxiv. 44. by Rev. *John Boggs,* of *Newcaftle* county.—This truly venerable man, and father in the gofpel miniftry, having difcharged with fidelity and reputation the feveral duties both of public and private life, through fuch a long feries of years, and fuftaining with chriftian patience, and uncommon refignation, the affliction of a very tedious illnefs, finally refted from his labours in confident affurance of a bleffed immortality, difcovering to the laft, that he partook of thofe divine confolations, which are but feldom experienced even by thofe who fleep in Jefus."

Mr. *William Davis* fettled firft at *Vincent*; he thence removed to *New Britain,* and had the joint care of that church with Mr. *Jofeph Eaton* till 1749, when Mr. *Eaton* died. Mr. *Davis* was the fucceffor there till his death on Oct. 3, 1768. The three firft paftors of this church, and many, if not moft of the conftituents, were likewife from the Principality*.

This year died the lively and excellent Mr. *John Harris,* paftor of the church at *Blaenau.* His colleague, Mr. *William Phillips,* died feven years before. Mr. *Harris* was one of the firft conftituents of the church in 1696. He had the honour to baptize his own father, and was very happy in his children. His eldeft fon *Harry,* was baptized at fixteen years of age, in 1714. His daughter *Lydia,* was baptized at fifteen, in 1716. And his youngeft fon *Morgan,* at fourteen, in 1720. who fucceeded his father in the paftoral care. Mr. *John Harris,* as is intimated be-

* See Mr. Edwards's Materials towards a Hiftory of the Baptifts in Pennfylvania, p. 48—52.

fore, was, in his day, the best writer of church records that has been found in the Principality, at least among the Baptists.

1738. *Hengoed*, 23d and 24th of May. The association letter complains of Arminianism up and down the country. The churches were mostly prosperous, yet not without sorrow. There was now a disagreeable contention at *Cilfowyr* about a successor to the late Pastor. Mr. *James Williams* had long been an acceptable help in the ministry, and part of the society thought it but right for him to succeed in the pastoral care. The other part thought that Mr. *David Thomas*, who had exercised his gifts with acceptance for ten or twelve years, though younger, being popular and acceptable, might be more beneficial to the church than an aged person. Tempers on both sides were too warm on the occasion. The association advised in the best manner they could, and a day of fasting and prayer was appointed through the churches on their account, with a due remembrance of others. Mr. *Thomas Matthias*, the pastor of *Rhydwilim*, preached from Jer. iii. 15. a text very suitable to those times, when pastors were removed every year.

On the 11th of June, this year, died the truly Rev. Mr. *Morgan Griffiths*, pastor at *Hengoed*, aged 69. He was highly respected of men, and much owned of God.

1739. *Llanwenarth*, 12th and 13th of June. The letter this year expresses joy and gladness, because prayers had been answered, advice received, contention had ceased, and reconciliation was made. *Cilfowyr* church had agreed to ordain the two ministers mentioned under last year, that they might administer the ordinances alternately. The two ministers agreed very well, the senior soon failed by age, and the work fell upon the junior. This letter, as several before had done, cautions the churches against suffering young men to go out in a disorderly way to preach. Brother *Griffith Jones* preached from 1 Cor. iv. 1, 2. and Brother *Hugh Evans* from Phil. iv 8. the latter part. This is the first time that we notice a MODERATOR mentioned in the letters; it has been the constant method since, and possibly it was before, for the minister who preached to be moderator. The persons, who signed here, were *Griffith Jones*, MODERATOR, *Thomas Matthias, Roger David, David Richard, Roger Walker, David Owen, Evan Thomas, David Lewis, Enoch Francis, Morgan Harris, David Thomas, Thomas David, Jacob Rees, Griffith Davis, Miles Harrys, Phillip Morgan, William Herbert*, and several who were not ministers. These are new names compared with the former.

The truly venerable Mr. *Caleb Evans*, of *Pentre*, died in April preceding this meeting, and was succeeded by his Brother, Mr. *John Evans*.

1740. *Cilfowyr*. Whitsun-week. The circumstances of the churches appeared hopeful, meeting houses had been built; ministerial gifts were increasing. This was a mercy, as so many pastors

tors had been lately removed. Brother *Morgan Harris* preached from Job. xxxiii. 23. and Brother *Hugh Evans* from 2 Kings li. 14. Mr. *Hugh Evans* always preached in English and repeated a little in Welsh.

Notice was taken above of the debate at *Hengoed* about 1730, and how it then issued. On the decease of the pastor, possibly Mr. *Winter's* friends wished and expected that he might succeed him, but there was a great majority against it. In order to keep together it was necessary to find a pastor that would suit both parties. They could fix upon no such person but Mr. *Griffith Jones*, the pastor at *Pen-y-fai*. It was thought an unkind act to separate a pastor and people, who had mutually loved each other so many years. But the case at *Hengoed* being so singular, the pastor was persuaded to remove, and the church suffered it to be so. They had however much trouble, before they were comfortably settled again. Mr. *Jones* and Mr. *Winter* were both of a peaceable temper, and agreed as well as could have been expected.

Year after year we have noticed the removal of several worthy pastors, who died in a good old age, after they had long and honourably served their generations. Alas! now a greater stroke was felt than any of late. Mr. *Enoch Francis* was removed in February preceding this meeting—A strong man, of a good constitution, about fifty years of age. This gave a shock to the whole association, and to all the country. He used to visit the churches once or twice a year, as he could make it convenient, and crouds flocked to hear him, professors and profane. Most of the persons whose names appear in the letter of last year signed here, and also *John Richard* and *John Morgan*; these two were helpers at *Cilfowyr*. *John David Nicholas*, and *Rees Jones*, were from Mr. *Francis's* church. As upon his decease they had no ordained minister, though several helpers; they agreed to ordain these two, and Mr. *Thomas David*, in May ensuing. Mr. *Jones* was then a promising young man. The other two were aged, and had been long in the ministry.

1741. *Blaenau*, 19th and 20th of May. This year's letter was long and good, containing reasons of joy and sorrow; queries from several churches answered, and complaint of young men going out to preach irregularly. Brother *David Owen* preached from 1 Cor. xvi. 10. and latter part, Brother *Foskett*, of *Bristol*, from 1 Thes. i. 5. This letter is signed by one or two and twenty ministers, all dead now. *Thomas Edwards*, *William Phillips*, *Charles Winter*, and *Morgan David*, were among them; also *Griffith Davis*, who was originally a member of, and then became Pastor at *Swansea*, where he had preached for sometime with acceptance; before he was settled in the pastoral care.

There was an attempt of late years to set up a SEMINARY *

* There was some kind of instruction given to young men at Pontypool as early as 1734, though I think, no proper Tutor till about 1736 or 1737.

at *Pontypool* for the benefit of candidates for the ministry. This year the following students Messrs. *Thomas Llewelyn* from *Hengoed*, *Morgan Edwards* from *Pen-y-garn*, *Edmund Watkins* of *Blaenau*, *Jonathan Francis* and *Timothy Thomas* of *Newcastle*, were all promising for the ministry. The prospect of a *Welsh* seminary, it is thought, was as flattering and animating then as ever it has been since; but it never could be brought properly to bear, though many young men have received considerable assistance at *Pontypool*.

1742. *Llanglyffan*. Whitsun-week. A long comprehensive letter at this time, which judiciously remarks many things in the course of Providence. The churches in peace, additions to most, and the means of grace plenty. Brother *Griffith Davis* and Brother *Hugh Evans* preached *. Several queries from different churches, upon discipline, answered. About this time *Llantrisaint* church was quite dissolved. Mr. *Thomas Williams*, who had been originally a member at *Hengoed*, ministered here for some years; but about this time he turned to the people called Quakers, and the few members belonging to *Usk* joined *Pen-y-garn*.

This year *Aberduar* church was constituted; it had been a large and extensive branch of *Newcastle* church. Two of the three ministers lately ordained, residing near the young church, were among the first constituents of it. Messrs. *Evan Saunders*, *John Thomas*, and *Timothy Thomas*, also had begun to exercise their ministerial talents about 1740. They likewise were in the young church, and *John David Nicholas*, an ordained minister, was at *Newcastle*, the old place. Thus the churches were still sixteen in number.

1743. *Cilfowyr*. Whitsun-week. A particular circumstance occasioned the Association to be here again so soon. It was no contention, but love †. The preceding letters mentioned the removal of many members by death; but this speaks of the decease of five ministers; Mr. *John Davis*, an aged, worthy assistant, at *Swansea*: Messrs. *Roger David* and *William Meredith*, at *Llanwenarth*; the first the pastor, the latter a very worthy and aged assistant; Mr. *William Herbert*, the colleague at *Trosgoed*, a very acceptable preacher, who had come from the Independants, and Mr. *Evan Saunders*.

Brother *Miles Harrys* preached from Jer. xv. 19. and brother *Evan Jenkins* in English and Welsh from 2 Tim. ii. 19. He was son to the late excellent Mr. *John Jenkins*, and father to the present worthy Dr. *Joseph Jenkins*, of *Wrexham*. We meet with no account of the numbers added to the churches till this year. Now it is noted that 125 were added, and near 50 lost by death. But this state of the numbers was inserted by an individual without any public consultation and general agreement. Near 20 years after the subject was debated and agreed to. About 23 signed

* The texts of 1742 are not in the copy from which this account is taken.

† This was the first association that ever the writer of this history attended.

here

here, among whom are *Griffith Thomas, Daniel Garnon, John James,* and *Timothy Thomas.*

About this time Mr. *Rees Jones* removed from *Aberduar* to the destitute church at *Pen-y-fai;* there was then at the former place only Mr. *Thomas David* an aged minister. Messrs. *John Thomas* and *Timothy Thomas* were now young in years, and in the ministry, but very acceptable at home and abroad; it was agreed to ordain them both this year.

1744. *Pen-y-garn.* Whitsun-week. The letter complains of Arianism and Arminianism. Mentions a mixture of comfort and sorrow, ministerial gifts increasing, and several queries which were answered. Brother *David Thomas,* of *Cilfowyr,* preached from 1 Chron. xxix. 1. and Brother *Hugh Evans* from Isaiah lxii. 6, 7. Mr. *Edmund Watkins* and Mr. *John Thomas* were among those who signed here.

Mr. *Miles Harrys* had now been a member of *Blaenau* above twenty years, and a preacher about eighteen. For ten years, or more, he had exerted himself much to promote the interest of religion in general, and particularly among his own denomination. He was of a very friendly and social turn; and corresponded with most of our Baptist ministers and others in *Wales;* with many in *England,* and some in *America.* He used to send to the FUNDEES in *London,* a very particular and friendly account of the Baptist ministers in *Wales,* their situation, who most useful, &c. and this he did annually, soon after each association, with short hints of the general state of the churches. For some years *Swanfea, Pen-y-fai, Blaenau,* &c. sent a letter to the Western Association, but none so often and so long as *Pen-y-garn.*

1745. *Pentre.* Whitsun-week. The churches were all in peace, and some addition to each. Brother *Thomas Edwards,* originally a member of *Blaenau,* but now pastor of *Llanwenarth,* preached from 2 Tim. ii. 15. and Brother *E. Jenkins* from Heb. xii. 15. This year died Mr. *James Williams,* the senior pastor at *Cilfowyr,* and Mr. *Thomas Matthias,* the pastor at *Rhydwilim,* both aged and honourable. This year *Llangloffan* formed into a regular church. It was a distant branch of *Rhydwilim,* and for many reasons it would have formed sooner, but out of regard to the aged pastor, it was deferred during his life. Mr. *John James* presided at *Rhydwilim,* and Mr. *David Richard* at *Llangloffau.*

1746. *Swansea.* Met at the usual time of the year. The state of the churches nearly as last year. Now 17 churches. Brother *Griffith Jones* preached from 2 Chron. xv. 7. and Brother *E. Jenkins* from Jude 21. The great deliverance from the Rebellion in the North is gratefully acknowledged, and a day of thanksgiving appointed. But this did not make so deep an impression on the minds of many as the deliverance in 1714 and 1715 did. The first of August, and the first Wednesday in every month, seldom ever failed to be mentioned in the letter for 20 years *.

* The paper from which this year's account is taken, does not mention the names of the persons who signed at this meeting.

This year Mr. *Thomas Edwards* died, at 34 years of age. He had been a few years paftor at *Llanwenarth*, a very acceptable minifter. Many lamented his death. He was fucceeded by Mr. *Caleb Harris*, who died in the Lord, May 27, 1792, in the 77th year of his age.

1747. *Brechfa*, belonging to *Trofgoed*, the fame time as before. Nothing very material in the ftate of the churches this year. Brother *Evan Thomas*, the paftor of *Molefton*, preached from John xxi. 17. and Brother *E. Jenkins* from 1 Thef. ii. 12. This year *Bethefda* formed, they were diftant members of *Hengoed*, *Pen-y-garn*, &c. This made the number of the churches eighteen, and fo they continued to 1768. Indeed one or two more formed before 1768, but were not till then received into the Affociation.

This year Mr. *Morgan Harris*, the paftor of *Blaenau* finifhed his race. He adorned the miniftry, but died about the age of 42. He left two fons, *John* and *Morgan*. The latter called to the miniftry at *Llanwenarth*, was ordained in 1779, to affift Mr. *Caleb Harris*. He fulfilled his miniftry with honour, acceptance, and fuccefs, till he died in 1790. This year Mr. *John Evans*, paftor at *Pentre*, died, aged 69, and was fucceeded by an affiftant of the fame name, though not related after the flefh. Alfo Mr. *Henry Morgan*, of *Llangloffan*, a very promifing young man. The people expected that he would have been their paftor for many years, but he finifhed his work at the age of 27. This was the firft year that JOSHUA THOMAS (now of *Leominfter*) appeared among thofe who figned the letter. The church at *Trofgoed* hitherto had no meeting-houfe; but a place was built in 1746, and called *Maes-y-berllan*, and henceforward we fhall give it that name.

1748. *Garth*, belonging to *Rock*. Whitfun-week. Nothing materially different in the ftate of the churches. Brother *Griffith Jones* preached from 1 Cor. ii. 2. and Brother *Hugh Evans* from 2 Cor. v. 20. The churches in peace, moft of them enjoyed plenty of means. The firft time the author of this Hiftory had the honour to write the circular letter was this year. After that it fell to his lot to write thofe of 1751, 1754, 1757, and 1770. It was then never mentioned in the letters who wrote them. The new names among thofe who figned this letter were, *Rees Evans*, *Thomas Davis*, *Evan David*, *James Lodwick* and *William Morgan*. The laft-named went that year to *Shrewfbury*, and ferved that church till he died in 1753.

Mr. *Roger Walker*, the paftor of *Rock*, finifhed his race a few weeks before this Affociation, though he earneftly wifhed to fee it.

1749. *Llanelli*. The ufual time. Brother *Griffith Thomas* preached from 2 Cor. v. 11. The fecond fermon was preached by Brother *David Thomas*, of *Cilfowyr*, and on the fecond day Brother *Griffith Jones* preached his farewell fermon from 2 Cor. xiii. 2. Soon after he failed for *Pennfylvania* with his family.

He

He settled in *Welsh Tract* church, but not as pastor, and there he died in 1754. His son *Morgan* returned to *England*, and now being called to the ministry, was many years pastor of the Baptist church at *Hempstead, Herts*. He now resides at *Hammersmith*, near *London*, as Principal of a respectable academy for the education of youth, and was distinguished by the college at *Providence, Rhode Island*, at their Commencement in September 1793, with the honours of L. L. D.

The Association Letter remarks that some of the churches in their letters did not mention their agreement with the Confession of 1689. But it was wished that they would not forget it in future.

There had been, a few years back, an exposition of the Church Catechism, published in *Welsh*, "By a minister of the "Church of England," in which he advanced twenty arguments for Infant Baptism. It was agreed at this meeting, that some of the ministers should think of an answer. Four or five of them were named, but not any individual fixed upon. Several entered on the subject, and among them Brother *Joshua Thomas* drew up a few hints, and was encouraged to go on, but the others did not proceed. This year Mr. *David Richard*, the pastor at *Llangloffan*, died. Many signed this letter, among them were *David Evan, Jonathan Francis, David Lewis*, and *John Evans*.

1750. *Moleston.* Same time. This letter mentions the Murrain among the cattle, which had been for years in *England*, and the two Earthquakes in *London*, &c. as a loud warning to *Wales*. A query from *Llanwenarth* was proposed, concerning the Trinity, some of whose members gave trouble upon that head, but it ceased in a few years. It was now agreed that what Brother *Joshua Thomas* had written on Baptism, in answer to the twenty arguments, should be printed, and that the churches should take the impression. The twenty arguments had been turned into *English*, and Dr. *Gill* also had written a short reply, and it was agreed to take part of the impression of his piece likewise. As *Moleston* was an *English* place in *Pembrokeshire*, the first sermon here was in that language, by Brother *E. Jenkins*, from Matt. xvi. 18. and the second by Brother *John Thomas*, in *Welsh*, from 2 Tim. iv. 5. Here no less than eight of the churches requested the next association to be with them.

The departure of Mr. *G. Jones* (the pastor at *Hengoed*) for *America*, naturally revived the old debate in that church. The consequence of which was an entire separation. Mr. *Winter*, and his friends, were about twenty-three. They agreed to form themselves into a church, and Mr. *Winter* to be their pastor. They built a meeting-house about four miles from *Hengoed*, and called it *Craigfargod*. Mr. *Winter* died in 1773. The church meets there still, but it is not in the association, being a general Baptist church, and it is the only one in all the Principality. Mr.

Jacob Isaac of *Moreton*, in *Devonshire*, was originally one of *Craig-fargod* Society, and there he began his ministry.

1751. *Hengoed*. Whitsun-week. It was now become a kind of an established custom to have an *English* sermon after the *Welsh* one. Mr. *Evan Jenkins*, pastor at *Wrexham*, did not belong to the Association, but he mostly attended, and preached at it in *English*, and gave a short repetition in *Welsh*, every year but three, from 1743 to 1751, both inclusive, and his assistance was acceptable. Here Brother *Griffith Davis* preached, and Brother *E. Jenkins*. This was the last time Brother *E. Jenkins* preached at these meetings. He died in March 1752. Our materials do not furnish us with the texts at this Association.

Early this year was published the *Welsh* answer to the twenty arguments for Infant Baptism, and in the summer, Dr. *Gill's* Answer to them came out, to which he added, "The Dissenters' Reasons for separating from the Church of *England**," The reasons for separating were then translated into *Welsh*, and bound up with the *Welsh* answer, written by Brother *Joshua Thomas*.

1752. *Aberduar*. The same time. It had been appointed at *Moleston* that the churches should not send less than two, nor more than three, messengers to the Association; and they were desired to send judicious persons who might be useful. They were here reminded of that appointment. Brother *Edmund Watkins* preached from Mark xvi. 15. and Brother *Caleb Harris* from Col. iv. 3, 4. both in *Welsh*. It was common ever since two sermons were preached at the Association to have one of them in *English*, but this year, and 1749, are exceptions.

1753. *Maesdurglwyd*, but belonging to *Olchon*. Whitsun-week. It was usual to have the meetings on Tuesday and Wednesday, but here it was on Wednesday and Thursday, that those who were at a distance might have more time to come. Brother *David Thomas*, of *Ciffowyr*, preached from 1 Tim. iv. 16. and Brother *Griffith Davis*, in *English*, from Eph. iii. 8. The churches in peace, the means plenty, ministerial gifts increasing, yet great complaints of declension in various respects.

1754. *Rhydwilim*. The usual time. Brother *Caleb Harris* preached from 2 Tim. ii. 25. and brother *Miles Harrys* from 1 Cor. xv. 34. These sermons were mostly in *Welsh*. The state of the churches similar to the preceding year. Complaint of not sending messengers to the Association.

1755. *Bethesda*. 21st and 22d of May. Here the eighteen churches are named in the front of the letter. Brother *Richard Jones* preached from 2 Tim. iv. 2. and brother *Hugh Evans*, in

---

* The whole Title of Dr. Gill's piece is as follows. "The Argument from Apostolic Tradition, in favour of Infant Baptism, with others, advanced in a late Pamphlet, called, the Baptism of Infants, a reasonable service, &c. considered. And also an Answer to a Welsh Clergyman's Twenty Arguments for Infant Baptism; to which are added, the Dissenters' Reasons for separating from the Church of England; occasioned by the said Writer."

English,

English, from 2 Tim. ii. 1. For several years back it had been proposed by some to keep the Association statedly on the second Wednesday and Thursday in June, as the Whitsun-week happened sometimes too early, before some had finished sowing barley, and before the horses were got strong to travel, and the grass grown sufficient for them. Others pleaded that the Whitsun-week was commonly a more leisure time, particularly for schoolmasters, &c. But here it was agreed, that in future the church where the Association was to meet should fix the time.

1756. *Pen-pont-Landyfyl*, belonging to *Newcastle*, 9th and 10th of June. Brother *Miles Harrys* preached from Rev. xiv. 6, 7. and Brother *Griffith Davis* from Acts v. 42. Notice taken of the earthquake at *Lisbon* and other places.—War with *France*.—It was agreed to print in *Welsh* Mr. *Wilson's* Scripture Manual on Baptism. When Mr. *Walker*, the pastor at *Rock*, died in 1748, his assistant, Mr. *Thomas Davis*, succeeded him in the ministry for some time. But the body of the church chose to look out for a successor in the pastoral office. Soon after they fixed upon Mr. *Richard Jones*, who had been among the Independents in the neighbourhood, but was convinced of Believers' Baptism, and soon after he submitted to it was ordained over them. He preached at *Bethesda* in 1755. This year, 1756, Mr. *Thomas Davis* died. He was a truly worthy man, though not a very popular preacher.

1757. *Llanwenarth*. Whitsun-week. Brother *Timothy Thomas* preached from 1 Cor ix. 16. Brother *Hugh Evans* also preached, but not having the letter of this year his text cannot be given; the passage Mr. *Timothy Thomas* preached on is inserted from the memory of the Author of these sheets, who happened to be at that meeting from *Leominster*. Now it was recommended to the members of the several churches to read the Confession of 1689 once or twice in the year. As that confession was referred to so often in the letters to and from the Association, it was necessary to know what it contained. That year I had translated a small Tract, entitled, "The Believers' Evidences for Heaven," and gave the copy to my Brother *Timothy* to print in *Welsh*, and with it he printed a sermon, which he had preached several years before, and had often talked of putting to press. It was upon 2 Pet. i. 10. He gave this title to it, "The White Stone;" alluding to Rev. ii. 17. This year died Mr. *Evan Thomas*, pastor at *Bridgewater*, He was originally a member at *Llanelli*; began to preach there about 1736; was at *Bristol* in 1740, under Messrs. *Foskett* and *Evans*; at *Warwick* and at *Birmingham* in 1742; and was at *Trowbridge* in 1744. Soon after he went there fifteen were baptized, and more expected to follow; he was much caressed for some time by the people of that church, but in 1746, he removed to *Bridgewater*, was there ordained in 1749, and died in 1757.

1758. *Llangloffan*. The first Wednesday and Thursday in June. Brother *David Owen* preached from Col. iv. 17. and Brother

ther *Hugh Evans* from 1 Cor. i. 23, 24. The first piece of advice in the letter runs thus: "As you have publickly submitted to the Gospel Baptism, and professed to believe the doctrine of Father, Son, and Holy Ghost, take care that this doctrine is held in its true scripture light. Though your reason cannot comprehend it in all its branches, yet faith hath her reason." There are in this letter, nine very good, plain, short articles of hortatory advice relative to doctrine and practice. The Newcastle church appeared too remiss in maintaining the doctrines of grace against Arminianism. That church had been about thirty years vexed with the general doctrines, by some neighbours who openly professed them. This year Mr. *John Thomas*, one of the pastors of *Aberduar*, removed, and took the pastoral care of the church at *Maes-y-berllan*, the pastor there resigning because of age and infirmities.

1759. *Blaenau.* The second Wednesday and Thursday in June. Brother *Evan Thomas* preached from Luke xii. 42, and Brother *Hugh Evans* from Acts xx. 24. It was agreed to print the Catechism, for the establishment of our youth in gospel principles. The general method of the Association to this time was, after the two sermons, to take some refreshment, then to read the preliminaries in *Welsh*, which are nearly the same as those of the Western Association in *England*, and then to read the letters from the churches. When that was done, one of the ministers was fixed upon to draw up the circular letter. After travelling, perhaps a long way, with but broken rest, the person fixed upon was under a necessity of sitting up most of, or all the night, that his letter might be prepared by about nine next morning, when it was to be read and corrected. As soon as it was ready each church was to find a person to write out a copy. The persons employed went to some retired place, one to read, and the others to write; some were very slow, and if there was but one so, all the rest were forced to wait. This was indeed very trying, and many of the copies were so imperfect as not to be easily read. Thus it was for many years. But the printing of the letter was a happy alteration.

This year died Mr. *William Thomas*, a worthy assistant at *Blaenau*.

1760. *Cilfowyr.* 11th and 12th of June. This year, for the first time, the Association Letter was printed. Now the care chiefly fell upon the pastor of the church, where the meeting was held, to prepare the body of the letter beforehand. The preamble of this letter doth not mention the Confession of 1689; but "Baptism; laying on of hands; eternal and personal election; that all the natural posterity of Adam are sinners through him; particular redemption; effectual calling; and perseverance in grace to the end." This is the first letter in which I have seen it thus expressed. The eighteen churches are here named, and the benefit of the association of churches is mentioned. Brother *Edmund Watkins* preached from Luke xiv.

23. and Brother *Benjamin Francis* from Tit. ii. 14.; the latter is paftor of the Baptift church at *Horfley, Gloucefterfhire*, fon to the late celebrated Mr. *Enoch Francis*, and was originally a member of *Swanfea*. The churches in peace; additions to moft, many to fome. Mr. *John James*, the paftor at *Rhydwilim*, dead. All the queries from the churches were not now inferted in the printed letters, as fome of them related to the internal affairs of the focieties, and would have been uninterefting to the public eye.

This year died Mr. *John Morgan*, an aged affiftant at *Cilfowyr*.

1761. *Pen-y-garn*. 10th and 11th of June. Here the Confeffion of 1689 is reaffumed. Brother *David Thomas*, member of a branch of *Newcaftle* church called *Ffynnon Henry*, ordained in 1747, to affift in the whole church, preached from Matt. xxii. 42. and Brother *Hugh Evans* from Rom. i. 16. The churches moftly enjoying comfortable circumftances, fome having large additions, and young men of promifing abilities for the miniftry. *Rhydwilim* had chofen a paftor from *Llangloffan* church, which had feveral, and could well fpare one. Three were ordained at *Cilfowyr* to help occafionally, and indeed feveral were now and then ordained at once in the large churches, where perhaps one or two might have ferved for the prefent, but this feems to have been done to prevent contention. Before the affociations in *England* and *Wales* began to *print* their letters, we had ufually the names of a confiderable number of perfons who figned them, but I HAVE OFTEN LAMENTED that we have now only the moderator's name, who, in the Principality, is always the minifter that preaches firft. The former way will be really helpful to our hiftorians. And I VERY MUCH WISH IT MAY AGAIN BE RESTORED IN ALL THE ASSOCIATIONS.

This year *Morgan Edwards*, M. A. failed to *Philadelphia*. He was originally a member at *Pen-y-garn*, and had now been in the miniftry about twenty years. Of his publications and labors in *America*, fee his Materials fo often referred to above.

1762. *Pentre* 9th and 10th of June. Brother *John Williams*, one of the Co-paftors at *Llangloffan*, preached from Col. i. 28. and Brother *Benjamin Francis* from 1 Pet. ii. 2. There had been fome talk before this of mentioning in the Letter the number added to each church, but the fenior minifters oppofed it, and pleaded that it looked like *David's* numbering the people. But this was eafily refuted by inftances from the Old and New Teftament; fo that at this meeting it was carried in the affirmative, without much offence to the few who oppofed it. The numbers ftand thus in the letter.

Churches 18, added 169, dead 30, excluded 9. Total increafe 130. They could not eafily guefs at the number of hearers, as they preached in fo many places ftatedly and occafionally.

This

This year died Mr. *James Lodwick*, one of the three ordained at *Cilfowyr* last year. He had been in the ministry there about 20 years, and was an acceptable preacher.

Pentre and *Rock* had been without proper meeting-houses from the beginning, till about 1760. The two places were opened this year, the one called after the old name *Pentre*, and sometimes *New Pentre*, the other is called *Dolau*, from the house near it where a meeting had been kept for many years.

1763. *Swansea*, 8th and 9th of June. Brother *David Thomas*, the pastor at *Rhydwilim* preached from Pf. li. 13. and Brother *Hugh Evans* from Eph. iv. 12, 13. and in the evening, Brother *Caleb Evans* (the late Dr. *Evans*) from Phil. ii. 1. All the churches in peace, and the means plenty, except at *Newcastle*, which had this year lost by death their co-pastors, Messrs. *John David Nicholas* and *Griffith Thomas*: and two others who assisted were removed, one by death, and another to *Aberduar* church. This was an uncommon stroke in one year; yet it was their mercy that two more were left in the church.

Added 94, dead 50, excluded 11, increase 33.

It is rather remarkable that from 1749 to 1763, not one of the pastors in this connexion died, but Mr. *John James*, of *Rhydwilim*.

1764. *Maes-y-berllan*, 6th and 7th of June. The Confession of 1689, is mentioned in the three last letters, but not in this, nor are the particular doctrines specified, yet a kind of a general sum of the whole is given. Brother *Lewis James*, the pastor at *Hengoed*, preached from 2 Tim. ii. 15. and Brother *Hugh Evans* from Hos. xiv. 5. The numbers are not in this letter, as in the two last, but this informs us that there had been an addition to all the churches but one, and it was thought the addition was double to that of last year.

Under 1737, some notice was taken of the debate that year concerning Laying on of hands. There happened to be another on the same subject in the church at *Aberduar* in 1743, though it was not of long continuance. The churches all held it except *Maes-y-berllan*, but some were very zealous for it, and others more moderate. *Cilfowyr* church was among the zealous ones, yet there were some members in that church, who were in doubt about the subject, and thought the others were rigidly zealous. The debate gradually extended itself. Brother *Timothy Thomas* the pastor at *Aberduar*, was zealous for the article. As the controversy spread, he drew up a few thoughts on it, and at a quarterly meeting in those parts, read it to the ministers present. And by some of them he was urged to print it. He put it to press this year, and also a Selection of hymns, which were of his own composing. Near the close of this year, *Glyn* church, in *Denbighshire*, was formed. It was a branch of *Wrexham* church, but situated at too great a distance comfortably to attend there.

1765. *Dolau, Radnorshire*, the first Tuesday and Wednesday in June. The Confession is here mentioned. Brother *George Rees*

preached

preached from 1 Pet. v. 2. and Brother *Benjamin Francis* from Mic. ii. 7. The churches all in peace, except one.

Added 121, dead 28, excluded 15, restored 7, increase 85.

Early this year came out an anonymous reply to Brother *Timothy Thomas*'s tract on Laying on of hands. The parties in this dispute disagreed about the address in the circular letter, which generally began thus, " The elders, &c. holding Baptism, upon faith and repentance, *Laying hands on the baptized*, &c." Those against Laying on of hands were by this address either excluded, or led to say an untruth. The debate grew warm here, but was conducted in tolerable good temper, of which I was a witness. My Brother *Timothy* was earnest for, and Brother *John Thomas* *, steady against the practice. They had been long fellow-labourers in the same church, but now the latter was at *Maes-y-berllan*, and they were both very worthy valuable men, and able ministers, though in this they could not agree. At this time the affair was left undecided. *Glyn* church had brought a letter, but as they were not under imposition of hands, the association would not then receive them into the connection.

This year died Mr. *David Owen*, the first and a worthy pastor of *Llanelli* church. He had been in that charge about thirty years, and in the ministry about forty years. The same year died Mr. *Samuel Griffiths*, a very promising young man, who was likely to settle at *Carleon*, in *Monmouthshire*, originally a member of *Moleston, Pembrokeshire*.

1766. *Llanelli*, 11th and 12th of June. Brother *Timothy Thomas* preached from Isa. xxvii. 13. and Brother *Hugh Evans* from Zech. xiv. 20. The churches tolerably in peace, though there were troubles in certain places. An addition to all of them but one.

Added 115, dead 48, excluded 27, restored 5, increase 45. The debate about the address was reassumed, and decided here. These words were inserted, after Laying on of hands, " *with others of the same sentiments, except Laying on of hands*," and thus it continues to this day, but a little abridged. This reconciled the association, but the debate still continued at *Cilfowyr*, and Brother *Timothy* published a defence of his tract upon the subject. This year a young man proposed for communion at *Cilfowyr*; but was rejected, because he could not acknowledge that Laying on of hands was a positive institution of Jesus Christ, though he was willing to submit to it as an usage in that church. This revived the dispute, and created uneasiness; the parties in the church proposed various terms on both sides, and thus they continued another year.

Before the association this year Mr. *John Duckfield* died. He was an assisting colleague to Mr. *D. Owen*, at *Llanelli*, and

---

* *Timothy Thomas* and *John Thomas* were not relatives they were both ordained together in 1743, and were colleagues till 1758, when the latter removed to *Maes-y-berllan*.

a man

a man of good understanding. Thus they lamented the loss of two ministers here since the last annual meeting. This year also died Mr. *Thomas David*, the senior minister at *Aberduar*. He was far advanced in years. The same year likewise died his son *Moses*, who was a baptist minister and resided at *Tarling*, in *Essex*, but was never pastor of any church.

1767. *Moleston*, 3d and 4th of June. Brother *Griffith Davis* preached from Col. i. 28. and Brother (the late Doctor) *Caleb Evans* from Col. iii. 2. Churches in about the same state as last year. Yet several complaints.

Added 97, dead 56, excluded 18, restored 5; increase 34.

The clause in the address this year runs thus: " With others, " who all of us agree with the articles contained in the Con- " fession of faith set forth in London in 1689." As the members at *Cilfowyr* could not agree cordially about Laying on of hands, those who were for it proposed, as the most likely way for peace, that those who were against it should depart in a friendly way, and form a church themselves, especially as there were among them an ordained minister and a deacon. So they did; hence the separation was in peace, and for the sake of peace. Both sides kept their temper remarkably well through the whole business, though it was long in agitation. Those who went off were about twenty-five, of whom Mr. *John Richard*, an aged ordained colleague, was one. They formed into a church this year, and chose him for their pastor. He had for his assistants Messrs. *William Williams* and *Thomas Henry*, both included in the above number. Thus peace was restored to this church, as well as to the association. And since that time this article has given no great trouble.

This year died Mr. *Rees Jones*, formerly an acceptable pastor at *Aberduar*; and Mr. *Samuel George*, at *Wantage, Berks*, originally a member at *Newcastle*.

1768. *Hengoed*. The 2d Wednesday and Thursday in June. Brother *David Thomas*, of *Newcastle*, preached from 2d Cor. iv. 5. and Dr. *Samuel Stennett* from Matt. xviii. 20. The churches in peace, with an addition to all of them but one. A branch of *Newcastle* church that was at a distance, in and near *Caermarthen*, peaceably formed into a church, and with the approbation of the mother church. Their pastor was Mr. *David Evans*, one of themselves, who had been long in the ministry in that branch to which they belonged. *Glyn* church, in *Denbighshire*, was here received into the connection. Mr. *William Williams*, one of the young church that separated from *Cilfowyr* last year, was a gentlemen of property; he built a meeting-house, upon his patrimonial estate, which was finished in March this year, and called it *Ebenezer*. This church was also received into the connection at the same time; which made the number 21.

This year, which afforded joy on the above accounts, was also a time of sorrow. My dear and worthy Brother, *Timothy*, now finished his active, though afflicted course. He was from
infancy

infancy of an unhealthy conſtitution, but unwearied, acceptable, and ſuccefsful in his miniſterial ſervices. He had been exerciſing his gifts before he was nineteen. I was informed, by a member of the church, that he began to preach the very day Mr. *Enoch Francis* died; and ſome were pleaſed to ſay that the unſpeakable loſs in the death of the latter was wonderfully made up in the former. Beſides what is mentioned above, he publiſhed a ſhort ſyſtem of divinity. Juſtification was the leading article in it, therefore he gave it this title, " The White Robe." Mr. *B. Griffiths*, paſtor at *Montgomery*, *Pennſylvania*, ſaw it, and in a letter to Mr. *Miles Harrys*, he ſays, " Pleaſe to give my chriſ-
" tian reſpects to Mr. *Timothy Thomas*. I value his *Welſh* book
" very much, and wiſh I could obtain one of them." He was Secretary to the aſſociation, and took the care of printing and diſtributing the circular letter. He died in the 48th year of his age, and was ſucceeded in the ſervice of the Aſſociation by his younger Brother, *Zechariah Thomas*, who, with two more, Mr. *David Davis*, and Mr. *David Saunders*, were ſometime after ordained in the church. Two of my Brother *Timothy's* ſons are now in the miniſtry. The eldeſt ſon, of the ſame name, lives where his father did; he has been ordained for ſome years: the other is Mr. *Thomas Thomas*, miniſter of the firſt-day church, which meets at *Mill-yard*, in *Roſemary-lane*, *London*. About five weeks before the death of Mr. *Timothy Thomas*, died Mr. *B. Griffiths*, juſt now named. And the ſame year Mr. *Rees Evans*, who had been paſtor at *Shrewſbury*, died at *Tewkſbury*, *Glouceſterſhire*; he was originally a member at *Pentre*. Mr. *John Richard*, the aged paſtor of the young church at *Ebenezer*, finiſhed his courſe; and ſo did Mr. *William Watkins*, at *Croſ-combe*, *Somerſet*, a member from *Blaenau*. After ſo many deaths this year the worſt is yet to come; the *Dolau* paſtor was excluded for immorality. This was a heavy ſtroke. He went to the people from whom he came. The numbers this year were,

Baptized 96, dead 57, excluded 12, reſtored 4, increaſe, 31.

1769. *Aberduar*. 14th and 15th of June. Brother *David Thomas*, of *Rhydwilim*, preached from 2 Cor. v. 14, and Brother *Benjamin Francis* from Rev. iii. 19. "Be zealous." The churches all in peace.

Baptized 99, dead 37, excluded 15, reſtored 3, increaſe, 50. I have no account of the death of any of our miniſters in the Principality this year. Mr. *Joſhua Thomas*, of *Lymington*, *Hampſhire*, a very promiſing young miniſter, who was formerly a member of *Rhydwilim*, and Mr. *Daniel Thomas*, of *Henley*, *Warwickſhire*, originally a member of *Pen-y-garn*, both ended their days in 1769. *Rhydwilim* loſt their paſtor by his own ſin. He was ſucceeded by Mr. *George Rees*, their preſent aged and worthy paſtor.

1770. *Chapel-y-ffin*, belonging to *Olchon*. 13th and 14th of June.

June. Brother *John Williams* preached from Acts xxvi. 22, 23; and Brother *Hugh Evans* from Mal. ii. 15.

Baptized 111, dead 45, excluded 20, restored 10, increase, 56.

In the letter is this paragraph; "*Wales* hath been noted in time past, not only for a desirable plenty of ministers among themselves, but also for sparing many worthy ones to supply destitute churches in *England, Ireland,* and *America*; but if God were to withhold ministerial gifts from the Ancient Britons, what nation under Heaven could help them?" Many who have laboured in *England* and *America* have been already mentioned in this history, and several have been ministers in *Ireland* also; as Mr. *Morgan Edwards*, now in *America*; Mr. *James Edwards*, his brother, for many years back at *Waterford*; the former from *Pen-y-garn*, the latter from *Lanwenarth*; also Mr. *Henry Phillips*, from *Pen-y-garn*, who was ordained at *Waterford*, and served the church in the *Back-lane, Dublin*, two years, and died in 1789, at *Sarum*. It was desired, at this meeting, that the letters from the churches should not be so long in future, as they took up much time to read them. No minister in the connexion died this year but Mr. *David Jones*, a promising young man, at *Llanwenarth*, who had been convinced of Believers' Baptism, while in the Independent Academy at *Abergavenny*, and joined the Baptists, for which he was expelled the Seminary. Mr. *James Drewett*, originally a member of *Pen-y-garn*, died at *Honiton, Devon.*

1771. *Pen-y-fai.* 12th, &c. June. Brother *William Williams* preached from 2 Cor. v. 11, and Brother *Benjamin Francis* from Pf. cxxvi. 6. The churches all in peace.

Baptized 102, dead 54, excluded 12, restored 11, increase, 47. A revival in several churches, others complaining. Noted in this letter, and that of last year, the great plenty of Bibles provided for *Wales*, more than ever before; a large impression in *London* in 1769, and another in *Caermarthen* in 1770; an inestimable blessing. Queries regarding discipline were proposed at most of the Associations.

This year died Mr. *William Williams*, who had been pastor at *Olchon*, but had resigned his office, and for many years assisted at *Maes-y-berllan*; and Mr. *Evan Edwards*, an aged and very worthy assistant at *Hengoed*. His son, Mr. *Watkin Edwards*, is there now, colleague with Mr. *Lewis James*. Mr. *Peter Evans*, originally a member at *Pentre*, but afterwards pastor at *Yeovil, Somerset*, died this year; a very worthy man, cousin to the late Dr. *Evans*, of *Bristol*.

1772. *Rhydwilim.* 10th and 11th of June. Brother *Griffith Davis* peached from 2 Cor. v. 20, and Brother *W. Williams*, of *Ebenezer*, from Heb. xii. 2. The churches all in peace, means plenty, additions to several, &c.

Baptized 105, dead 34, excluded 27, restored 11, increased 56. It was agreed to reprint the Catechism for youth.

A new

A new church formed at *Carleon* in 1771, and another at *Uſk* in 1772, both in *Monmouthſhire*, joined the Aſſociation this year. The latter was partly at *Llangwm*, the ancient place, and branch was at *Llantriſaint* in former years. Now the churches were 23.

I do not recollect that any miniſter belonging to the Aſſociation died this year but Mr. *Jacob Rees*; he ſucceeded Mr. *W. Williams* at *Olchon*, but had reſigned his office many years, and was very aged. This year alſo Mr. *Caleb Evans*, a native of *Pentre* died, near *Charleſtown, South Carolina*; he was another couſin of the late Dr. *Evans* of *Briſtol*.

1773. *Betheſda*. 9th and 10th of *June*. Brother *John Williams* preached from Matt. xxii. 4. and brother *Hugh Evans* from Zech. i. 5. Mr. *David Thomas*, of *Cilfowyr*, was appointed to preach at this meeting, but he died before the time. Mr. *Hugh Evans*'s ſermon was very ſuitable to the providence, and at requeſt it was printed in Engliſh and Welſh. Mr. *David Thomas* was a worthy miniſter of deſerved repute. There is no account of the additions, &c. in this letter. It was filled up with other matter, particularly with ſome reſolutions agreed upon reſpecting an application to parliament for the further relief of Proteſtant Diſſenters. It was here agreed, That in future the circular letter ſhould be prepared by the miniſter where the Aſſociation might meet. The churches not all quite peaceable. A new church was formed at *Salem*, in *Carmarthenſhire*; the conſtituents were members from *Rhydwilim, Cilfowyr*, and *Carmarthen* churches, but being conveniently ſituated to form one ſociety, they had proper diſmiſſions cheerfully granted them.

1774. *Ebenezer*. 8th and 9th of *June*. Brother *Edmund Watkins* preached from Acts xx. 26, 27. and Brother *Benjamin Francis* from 1 Cor. xv. 58.

Baptized 333, dead 57, excluded 16, reſtored 8, increaſe 268.

Many were baptized in ſome of the churches, but the peace of one or two of them was diſturbed, as will ſoon appear. The letter this year was a very good one, intended to caution, direct, &c. The additions this year exceeded any one before. No miniſter in the connexion died this year, if I recollect rightly, but Mr. *Thomas Lewis*, originally a member at *Pen-y-garn*, who ſettled ſome years at *Tiverton*, was afterwards paſtor of the church at *Exeter*, and departed this life on December the 4th, after this aſſociation, aged 44. He was an affectionate uſeful miniſter, peculiarly attentive to young chriſtians, and could not be known without being loved.

1775. *Uſk*. 14th and 15th of *June*. Brother *William Williams* preached from Hoſea vii. 9. and Brother *Hugh Evans* from Heb. xii. 22, 23. Brother *Thomas Hiller*, of *Tewkſbury*, providentially there, preached in the evening from Luke viii. 35. Many of the additions, this year and laſt, were to the young church in and near *Carmarthen*, and to the mother church at *Newcaſtle*, about that time and ſince, called *Pant-têg*, from a new meeting-houſe of that name. Many of thoſe who had been baptized

tized were young, and the old members looked upon them as inexperienced and flashy; in return, they looked on the old as formal and lifeless. Thus they made each other uncomfortable, and probably there was some truth, and some error on each side. The uneasiness respected neither doctrines nor morals in general; but was about the method of singing. The consequence of it was, the young people, at both places, separated in March and April, preceding this Association, and formed two churches; but the ministers and messengers who met at *Usk* disapproved of the cause and manner of the division, and therefore would not receive them into the connexion; they were advised to return to their churches, and be reconciled. So it was then left.

This year baptized 278, dead 66, excluded 17, restored 19, received by letters 6, dismissed 3, increase 217.

This year died Mr. *John Evans*, the pastor at *Pentre*, a judicious man; and Mr. *Charles Harris*, at *Bridgwater, Somerset*, originally a member at *Pen-y-garn*.

1776. *Pant-têg*. 12th and 13th of *June*. Brother *Joshua Thomas*, of *Leominster*, preached the preceding evening from Psal. xlii. 5. On the morrow, Brother *John Thomas* preached from Deut. xxxiii. 3. and Brother *Benjamin Francis* from Phil. i. 27. Baptized 260, dead 55, excluded 27, restored 16, dismissed 1.—Increase 193. Four-and-twenty churches sent messengers to this assembly, of whom three were without pastors, but all had preachers and helps. At this time, and often before, the churches were advised to be prudent and orderly in sending young men into the ministry, and in receiving those who were beginning to preach. It was agreed to print the preliminaries of the Association, and to send a few copies to each church for information. This year, after the Association, the four following ministers died, Mr. *Philip Morgan*, formerly pastor at *Maesy-berllan*, aged about 83. He had been long afflicted. Mr. *Griffith Davis*, pastor at *Swansea*, aged 77; a worthy man. Mr. *Miles Harrys*, pastor at *Pen-y-garn*, aged 76. He had been formerly a very public man, useful and acceptable. He generally sent a letter from his church to the Western Association till near the last. At times letters were sent to this body from *Swansea*, *Pen-y-fai*, and *Blaenau*, as a remembrance of the former connexion in the last century. The fourth was Mr. *Isaac Jones*, son of Mr. *Rees Jones*. Mr. *Rees Jones* was one of the three who having been a long time assistants, were ordained this year at *Pentre*, to succeed the late pastor. The other two were Messrs. *John Evans* (a kinsman of Dr. *Caleb Evans*), and *Morgan Evans*. Mr. *Isaac Jones* was a very promising young man. Towards the close of life, he supplied in a probationary way at *Lynn, Norfolk*; but his health being impaired, he returned to *Wales*, and the affliction ended in death.

This year, by the friendly interposition of the late Dr. *Llewelyn*, the Gentlemen Managers of the Particular Baptist Fund in London were pleased to allot a sum of money to encourage a
million

mission into *North Wales,* particularly the counties of *Merioneth, Carnarvon* and *Anglesea;* in those counties, and part of *Denbighshire,* the Baptists were comparatively unknown. Mr. *David Evans,* the pastor at *Dolau,* made the first attempt this year, and was encouraged to repeat his visit. After that the ministers went from the South commonly two at a time. At this Association Dr. *Llewelyn* lodged part of the money in the hands of Mr. *Williams* of *Ebenezer,* and a sum in my hands, and wished us to do what we could in the affair; but as my residence was so far out of the way, the whole business at length devolved on Mr. *Williams,* and he exerted himself much to promote the design.

1777. *Carleon.* 11th and 12th *June.* Brother *George Rees* preached from 2 Cor. v. 18. and Brother *Hugh Evans* from Luke xii. 43. This was the last time Mr. *Evans* honoured this Association; and the first time was in 1736, so that he rendered his kind service to this Association above forty years. This year the numbers stood thus: Baptized 216, dead 67, excluded 41, restored 11, Increase 119. Brother *Benjamin Francis* preached in the evening from 1 Cor. ii. 2. *Glyn, Salem* and *Swansea* without pastors. Mr. *Daniel Garnon* died this year, an aged ordained minister at *Llangloffan,* but had lately removed his communion to *Ebenezer.*

The churches had been previously desired to give their opinion at this meeting whether it would be expedient for Brother *Joshua Thomas* to print the history of the Welsh Baptists in their native language; that the work might be laid aside, or set forward, as he could not think of printing it without their approbation. The result was, that every church not only gave assent to the eligibility of the design, but contributed more or less to help it on.

The new church formed in 1776, at *Wern,* now *Trosnant,* near *Pontypool,* was received into the connexion, Mr. *Miles Edwards* pastor, son of the late Mr. *T. Edwards,* pastor at *Llanwenarth.* Those who separated from *Newcastle* and *Carmarthen* were not admitted into the connexion, but were advised to re-unite. The mission to the North continued; sometimes one minister went, commonly two.

1778. *Salem.* Third Wednesday and Thursday in *June.* Brother *Thomas Phillips,* pastor at *Carleon,* preached from Acts xv. 16, and Brother *Benjamin Francis* from Luke x. 2. Baptized 159, dead 54, excluded 55, restored 11, Increase 61. The two separated societies continued so yet, and wished to be received into the Association as two churches. The subject was then considered afresh; and it appeared, that after so many years trial, the best way to promote peace and love was, to continue separate; and both churches were received. That, near *Newcastle,* was called *Graig,* from a new meeting-house they had erected: That in *Carmarthen, Priory-street,* their place of worship being in the street of that name. Another young church formed in 1777, called now *St. Nicholas,* after the name of the parish, was received into the connexion. This made the number 28.

This year died Mr. *John Price*, a young candidate at *Llanwenarth*. The Tuesday evening Brother *David Davis* preached from Rev. i. 13. The constituents of the church at *St. Nicholas* were 24, all baptized since the last Association. This year, and two years before, the names of all the ministers who engaged in prayer are inserted.

1779. *Glyn, Denbighshire.* 9th and 10th of *June*. This was in the North, though the church originated from *Wrexham*. In April preceding the Association, Mr. *David Evans*, the first who went on this mission, publicly baptized two in a river in *Anglesea*, and a few days before this meeting ten more were baptized in that island. Hence, a number from that, and other counties in the North, came to *Glyn* to see what an Association was, and they were desirous to have as many sermons as possible. Brother *John Williams*, the pastor at *Llangloffan*, preached from John i. 1—3. and Brother *Samuel Medley*, of *Liverpool*, in English, from Zech. ix. 16, 17. repeated in Welsh by Brother *T. Phillips*; after a little refreshment, Brother *Stephen Davis*, pastor of the new church at *Carmarthen*, preached from Mat. xvi. 24. and Brother *George Rees* from Acts xi. 21. This year baptized 161, dead 40, excluded 32, restored 16, Increase 105. From this meeting Messrs. *Stephen Davis*, of *Carmarthen*, and *David Jones* and pastor of *Pen-y-garn*, went to *Anglesea*, where, on the 20th of *June*, three more were baptized; and on that day they formed the fifteen into a church, and administred the Lord's supper to them. The church is called *Ebenezer*.

Previous to the *Glyn* meeting, a book had been printed in Welsh, containing some things regarding the Trinity, which many supposed heterodox. In this letter, the Association testified their disapprobation of them, as a Baptist was supposed to be the author of the book. From that time there have been imprudent expressions introduced upon an article not understood. After this Association died Mr. *David Jones*, formerly the pastor at *Wrexham*, by whose ministry the *Glyn* church had been raised. He was originally a member of *Moleston*. In 1779, died also Mr. *John Hopkins*, of *Swansea*, and Mr. *John Griffith*, of *Rhydwilim*, both aged useful helps.

1780. *Llanwenarth*. 13th, 14th, and 15th of *June*. Last year they began to read the letters from the churches on the Tuesday afternoon, that Wednesday might be mostly employed in praying and preaching. Here the churches are all named in the address; the *Anglesea* church formed last year being now admitted, made the number 29. All the societies in peace. Brother *Zechariah Thomas* preached from Gal. vi. 14. and Brother *Caleb Evans*, of *Bristol*, from 1 Tim. i. 15. After proper refreshment, Brother *Benjamin Francis* preached from 1 Thess. ii. 13. and Brother *David Evans* from Eph. i. 23. Baptized 166, dead 94, excluded 31, restored 19, Increase 60.

This

This year died Mr. *David Owen*, of *Llanelli*, son to the late pastor there, of the same name; and Mr. *Francis Lewis*, pastor at *Newbury, Berks*, originally a member of *Llanwenarth*.

1781. *Llangloffan*. 13th and 14th of *June*. Tuesday evening, Brother *William Williams*, of *Ebenezer*, preached from Heb. iii. 7, 8; and on Wednesday, Brother *John Thomas* from Jer. iii. 23, and Brother *Benjamin Francis* from Matt. xxv. 21. Baptized 202, dead 77, excluded 51, restored 32, received by letters 4, Increase 110. A wish was expressed to have the Confession of Faith reprinted. Some churches very prosperous. A meeting-house was wanted in *Anglesea*; the churches were desired to contribute towards it, and send their collections to Brother *William Williams*, of *Ebenezer*; Brother *David Evans*, of *Dolau*; or Brother *David Jones*, of *Pen-y-garn*, in or before October next. This year died Messrs. *Richard Watkins*, of *Penyfai*, and *Daniel Thomas* of *Rhydwilim*, two acceptable assistants.

1782. *Blaenau*. 12th and 13th of *June*. Brother *James Thomas*, the pastor at *Pant-têg*, formerly *Newcastle*, preached Tuesday evening; his text is not mentioned in the letter; and Wednesday, Brother *George Rees* from Zech. iii. 4. and Brother *Benjamin Francis* from Luke xiv. 23. Here the 29 churches are named and numbered. Disorders in some churches were complained of. Baptized 196, dead 68, excluded 29, restored 22, Increase 121.

1783. *Cilfowyr*. 4th and 5th of *June*. *Morgan Rees*, the pastor at *Llanelli*, preached Tuesday evening from 1 Pet. ii. 4. and Wednesday, Brother *Miles Edwards*, pastor at *Trosnant*, from Psal. xciii. 5. and Brother *Thomas Thomas*, then of *Pershore, Worcestershire*, but now at *Mill-yard, London*, from Rom. v. 11. Churches in peace. Additions to most. Baptized 180, dead 89, excluded 36, restored 22, Increase 77. This year, both *North* and *South Wales* sustained a great loss in the death of the deservedly respected THOMAS LLEWELYN, L. L. D. He was a cordial friend to his native country, both in a civil and religious sense. The letter of this year records the death of Mr. *William Hughes*, a worthy colleague in the ministry at *Llanelli*; and also the decease of Mr. *Evan Thomas*, the faithful and aged pastor at *Moleston*, of whom it is noted, that he had attended the Association near fifty years, and it was believed had been absent but once in all that length of time.

1784. *Pen-y-garn*. The 2d Wednesday and Thursday in *June*. The letters were read here upon Tuesday afternoon. Peace in the churches. The death of useful members is lamented, particularly of Mr. *David Thomas*, the respectable pastor at *Pant-têg*, for many years. He came from the Independents about forty years before. He had been exercised with many trials, and bore fruit in old age. He was a judicious man. By appointment he preached at a quarterly meeting in *Pembrokeshire*, May 1779, from Gal. ii. 16. The ministers then present requested him to favour them with the discourse; he complied; the subject is Justification. It was preached, and is printed in Welsh. This year

year also died Mr. *Thomas Davis*, the pastor at *Fairford*, in *Gloucestershire*; he served that church with great acceptance above forty years. He was originally a member of *Pentre*. The same year died Mr. *Thomas David* of *Cilfowyr*, an acceptable assistant there. At this meeting Brother *David Evans*, of *Graig*, preached from Zech. ix. 9, and Brother *Caleb Evans*, of *Bristol*, from Psal. cxix. 129. In the afternoon, Brother *John Richard*, a colleague at *Graig*, from Luke ii. 10, and Brother *Henry David*, a colleague at *Llangloffan*, from John i. 14. and after him Brother *Benjamin Morgan*, now pastor at *Bridgewater, Somerset*, from Zech. iv. 2. Baptized 295, dead 86, excluded 53, dismissed 3, restored 26, Increase 179. The churches were advised not to receive strangers into communion without a letter from the churches to which they belonged, or some certainty of their being orderly members.

By this time the Baptists were increasing in *North Wales*. A tolerably large meeting-house was erected chiefly in 1781, near the centre of *Anglesea*. A considerable part of the money to defray the expence was procured in *South Wales*, by the influence of Mr. *Williams* of *Ebenezer*, Dr. *Llewelyn* of *London*, and Mr. *David Evans* of *Dolau*. Mr. *Williams* exerted himself honorably in this affair, and, difficulties being surmounted, the house was named as his own place of worship is, viz. *Ebenezer*.

1785. *Graig*, near *Newcastle.*. 2d. Wednesday and Thursday in *June*. Tuesday evening, Brother *Zechariah Thomas* preached from Cant. ii. 9. Wednesday, Brother *David Jones*, of *Pen-y-garn*, from 2 Tim. i. 10. and Brother *Thomas Thomas* from John viii. 32. Peace increasing in the societies. Three young churches received into fellowship: *Beaumaris* in *Anglesea*; *Roe* on the borders of the counties of *Carnarvon* and *Denbigh*; and *Twyngwyn* in *Monmouthshire*. The churches now 32, all named in the letter. Baptized 332, dead 71, excluded 56, dismissed 1, restored 21, Increase 225. The letter mentions the death of Mr. *Timothy Thomas*, one of the colleagues at *Graig*, who died in 1784, but after the Association at *Pen-y-garn*. This year also died Mr. *William Harris*, the pastor at *Glyn*, a very promising young man, originally a member of *Priory-street, Carmarthen*.

1786 *Pentre*. 14th and 15th of *June*. Tuesday evening, Brother *Miles Edwards* preached from Psal. xxxvi. 7. Wednesday, Brother *Henry David*, of *Llangloffan*, from Jer. xv. 19. Then Brother *Caleb Evans*, of *Bristol*, in English, from 1 John iv. 10, whose discourse was briefly repeated in Welsh by *Joshua Thomas* of *Leominster*. After that Brother *George Rees* preached from 2 Cor. v. 4. The churches at *Moleston, Glyn*, and others, complained that they were as sheep without shepherds. Baptized 410, including the new churches, dead 93, excluded 59, restored 29, dismissed 5, received by letter 5, Increase 287. New churches this year, *Ystrad-dafodog*, in *Glamorganshire*, raised up providentially without much connexion with any church. *Nevin*, in *Carnarvonshire*; they soon built two good meeting-houses there

there, one in the town, and the other at a proper distance in the country, which they called *Salem*. Another new church in the same county near *Creckith*; they likewise erected a meeting-house and called it *Horeb*. And a fourth church in *Merionethshire*; their new place of worship was called *Ramoth*, a few miles north-west of *Harleigh*. Mr. *David Morris*, who afterwards died at *Carmarthen*, was of great service in the ministry, and in erecting meeting houses at *Nevin* and *Salem*, then but one church: and Mr. *David Hughes* was active and successful in the two churches *Horeb* and *Ramoth*. *Ystrad*, *Nevin*, *Horeb*, and *Ramoth*, sent letters to this convention, and were all admitted into the connexion. And after the Association, the same summer, another church was formed at *Newbridge*, in *Denbighshire*, between *Wrexham* and *Oswestry*. The constituents of it were members from the two churches at *Wrexham* and *Glyn*, both of whom gave their consent and approbation to this incorporation. Mr. *Jenkin Davis*, who had been for some time at *Beaumaris*, in *Anglesea*, removed to the pastoral care of this new church. This year died Mr. *Seth Morris*, who had been lately settled pastor at *Ebenezer*, in *Anglesea*; and, before the end of the year, Mr. *John Thomas*, pastor at *Maes-y-berllan*, and Mr. *William Williams*, his colleague. Breach upon breach. This year also died Mr. *David Evans*, at *Bigglswade*, *Bedfordshire*, originally a member at *Moleston*, *Pembrokeshire*. Churches now 36 in number.

1787. *Priory-street*, *Carmarthen*. Second Wednesday and Thursday in *June*. Here the letters were read Tuesday evening, in order to have more time for preaching next day. The state of the churches various. Some very peaceable and prosperous, but others not so. Ministerial gifts increasing in several places, which also is mentioned in the letters most years. Wednesday, Brother *David Jones* preached from Mal. i. 11, and Brother *Thomas Thomas*, then of *Pershore*, from 1 John ii. 3; and in the afternoon Brother *Job David*, of *Frome*, originally a member of *Pen-y-fai*, from 2 Cor. iv. 17. and Brother *Timothy Thomas*, of *Aberduar*, from Isaiah liii. 10. Baptized 402, dead 71, excluded 72, restored 28, received by letters 3, Increase 290. New churches received here were, *Llanfachreth*, near *Holyhead*, in *Anglesea*; *Newbridge* above mentioned; *Neuadd*, in *Brecknockshire*, which had been a distant branch of *Maes-y-berllan*, now peaceably formed for conveniency; and the *Engine*, *Glamorganshire*, organized some time before, though not in the connexion. This made the number of churches 40.

Agreed, that, if contention should arise in any church likely to make a breach in it, none of our ministers should either preach to them, or in any way encourage a separation among them, till the matter be first considered at the Association, or at a quarterly meeting, or at a meeting of ministers called for the purpose. Reported that a new impression of a POCKET BIBLE, in Welsh, with references, like *Cann's*, was in the press. Faithful ministers were requested to go and assist where the harvest was great, but the labourers few. Thanks were voted to Mr. *Benjamin Francis* for his WELSH HYMNS FOR PUBIC WORSHIP. This year died Mr. *Rees Jones*, the fenior paftor at *Pentre*; and Mr. *John Morgan*, an aged, ufeful affiftant at *Maes-y-berllan*; and Mr. *David Evans*, the paftor at *Thorn, Bedfordfhire*, originally a member of *Aberduar*, a valuable young man, aged 31.

1788. *Llannerchmedd*, in *Anglefea*, belonging to *Llanfachreth*, 2d Wednefday and Thurfday in *June*. In this country, they were eager to have as much preaching as poffible. Several of the minifters came about 12 on the Tuefday. Brother *Morgan Rees*, paftor at *Pen-y-garn*, (Mr. *David Jones* was removed to *Graig*), preached from Hab. iii. 9. and Brother *David Powel*, from Matt. xvii. 26. The fame evening, Brother *Gabriel Rees* preached from Luke xxiv, 26, and Brother *Benjamin Phillips*, paftor at *Salem*, in *Carmarthenfhire*, from Exod. iii. 3. Wednefday, Brother *David Evans*, of *Dolau*, preached from Rev. i. 20. and Brother *Benjamin Davies*, in Englifh and Welfh, from John iii. 19. and Brother *Henry David* from Eph. iii. 8. This letter takes an affectionate and refpectful notice of the death of Mr. *Evan David*, the worthy paftor of *Bethefda*, where he ferved faithfully near forty years; he was firft a member of *Rhydwilim* then of *Llangloffan*. To whom muft be added, Mr. *James Thomas* an acceptable fucceffor to the late paftor at *Pant-tég*, who died in the prime of life; and Mr. *Samfon Davis*, an affiftant at *Llanelli*. He came from the Independents, and had been in the miniftry many years. Baptized 513, dead 90, excluded 80, reftored 44, difmiffed 19, Increafe 368. After the letters were read, Brother *David Evans*, paftor at *Cilfowyr*, preached from Pfal. cxlix. 2. and Brother *Timothy Thomas* from Ifa. xiv. 32. The circular letter was drawn up by Mr. *Thomas Morris*, the paftor.

New churches this year. *Llandyfaen*, near *Llandilo*, in *Carmarthenfhire*, a church confifting of forty-fix members the firft year. The *New Houfe*, in *Back-lane, Swanfea*: This was rather an unhappy feparation from the old church in that town. Mr. *Lewis Thomas*, the fenior paftor at *Cilfowyr*, was removed to his long home after this Affociation. Mr. *Rees David*; paftor of a Baptift church at Norwich, originally a member of *Peny-fai*, died this year. He was a fenfible and popular young man.

As the churches were now become fo numerous and fo diftantly fituated, the letter propofed to their confideration, whether it would not be advantageous to have more than one Affociation.

1789. *Maes-y-berllan*, 9th and 10th of June. The addrefs in the circular letter, ever fince 1735, expreffed an approbation of the Confeffion of Faith republifhed in 1689, except twice or three times, when, nevertheless, the general contents of it were expreffed without mentioning the Confeffion. But, ever fince 1779, there had been fome whifperings about the commonly received doctrine of the Trinity; and fome objections to figning any formularies compofed by fallible men. But ftill the addrefs was in fubftance the fame, and the Confeffion fully referred to. At this meeting
the

the subject was debated. Part of the assembly were for the ancient method, and part for altering it. The form of words was considerably changed. Some were pleased, and others bore with it.

Tuesday evening, the letters were read; the churches mostly in peace; additions to all but two. Baptized 603, dead 87, excluded 101, restored 50, Increase 465. Wednesday, Brother *William Williams*, of *Ebenezer*, near *Cardigan*, preached from Neh. viii. 2; and Brother *Caleb Evans*, of *Bristol*, from Acts xv. 29. In the afternoon, Brother *Gabriel Rees* preached from 1 Tim. vi. 6. and Brother *Benjamin Francis* from Rom. vi. 15. Three new churches were received; *Aberystwyth*, in the north of *Cardiganshire*; *Nottage*, formerly a remote branch of *Pen-y-fai*; and *Bryn-Salem*, whose constituents had long been distant members of *Pen-y-fai* and *Swansea*, and supplied from both places.

About the close of 1788, came out in Welsh, a tract upon Infant Baptism, by Mr. *Benjamin Evans*, a minister near *Cardigan*; and in 1789, an Answer to it by Mr. *William Richards*, of *Lynn*, *Norfolk*, originally a member of *Salem*, in *Carmarthenshire*, well acquainted with his native language, and with the Baptismal controversy. Mr. *Benjamin Evans* published a Rejoinder; and Mr. *Richards* replied again. It was agreed that next year the Association should be divided into three, and the churches were desired to consider to which they would respectively join. This separation was to be made in love, with a view to enlarge and establish the interest of Christ.

1790. *Dolau*, in *Radnorshire*. 9th and 10th of June. Tuesday evening, the letters were read; most of the churches in peace; great additions to some. Baptized 544, dead 84, excluded 101, restored 42, received by letter 7, dismissed 1, Increase 407. Wednesday, Brother *Edmund Watkins* preached from Luke xiv. 22, 23; and Brother *Benjamin Francis* from Phil. iii. 16. In the afternoon, Brother *John Evans*, of *Roe*, preached from 2 Cor. iv. 7; and Brother *David Jones* from Isaiah lx. 7; and, lastly, Brother *Joshua Thomas*, of *Leominster*, from Joshua xxi. 45.

The Thursday is always employed in reading the circular letter, and in attention to other business; so that, in fact, the association continues three days. Being present, I was admitted into the convention on Thursday. There was nothing said about the manner of the address so much debated the year before; yet, in the printed letter, it is considerably altered from that of last year. The Confession of 1689 is referred to better than it was the year before, yet not quite in the former manner. I took the liberty to move the reprinting of that Confession in Welsh, and the revising the first edition which is very scarce and incorrect. The moderator readily seconded the motion; and I do not recollect to have heard one negative voice. Hence it was inserted in the letter, that the members of each quarterly meeting in the connexion should consider among themselves whether it would be right to print it as it is, only revising the language, or to make any alterations, and then

then send their thoughts to Brother *Joshua Thomas*, of *Leominster* who is appointed to correct it. And now I remark, upon the whole, there has of late years been some difference in the expressions of certain persons upon the confessedly deep and mysterious doctrine of the adorable Trinity. Ministers used words, perhaps without caution, then one accused the other, probably beyond the real guilt, and there has been some improper warmth on each side. Several attacks have been made upon the peace and orthodoxy of our brethren in the Principality through the course of this century; but they have hitherto been mercifully preserved from many errors that prevail in other places; may they still be kept sound in doctrine, and circumspect in conduct.

The new church at *Neath, Glamorganshire*, was admitted this year, making the number forty-six; and the whole were formed into THREE ASSOCIATIONS, thus,

The *Northern*, consisting of the churches at *Glyn, Newbridge, Denbighshire; Ramoth, Merionethshire; Horeb, Salem,* and *Roe, Carnarvonshire; Beaumaris, Ebenezer,* and *Llanfachreth, Anglesea:* nine in all.

The *Eastern*, in South Wales. *Dolau* and *Pentre, Radnorshire; Builth, Maes-y-berllan,* and *Chapel-y-ffm, Brecknockshire; Llanwenarth, Blaenau, Peny-garn, Trosnant Twyngwyn, Usk, Caerleon,* and *Bethesda,* in *Monmouthshire; Hengoed, Ystrad-dafodog, St. Nicholas, Nottage, Pen-y-fai,* and *Neath,* in *Glamorganshire:* nineteen in all.

The *Western* in South Wales. *Bryn-Salem, Engine, Swansea, Back Lane* in *Swansea, Glamorganshire; Llanelli, Priory Street, Porthtywyll, Salem, Rhydwilim, Graig, Pant-tég, Aberduar,* and *Llandyfaen, Carmarthenshire; Moleston Llangloffan, Ebenezer,* and *Cilfowyr, Pembrokeshire;* and *Aberystwyth, Cardiganshire;* these are eighteen in all.

N. B. The new church at *Neuadd* is now called *Builth,* and *Olchon* is called *Chapel-y-ffm; Olchon* is in *Herefordshire, Chapel-y-ffm* in *Brecknockshire,* yet but about two miles distant from each other. The latter have a meeting-house, the former never had a proper one.

In the letter, it is observed, that this division of the churches into three associations was effected in love and harmony; and that, should circumstances require it in future, they will all meet by deputies in a General Assembly, as well to advise and assist each other, as to brighten the golden chain of fellowship; and, should ministers or members of one Association go to another, they shall for that time enjoy equal privileges with those who are real members. It was agreed that each Association should have liberty to chuse whom they pleased to preach, out of all the three conventions. The first Association to be at *Hengoed,* the first Wednesday and Thursday in June 1791; Brother *David Evans,* of *Dolau,* to preach; in case of failure, Brother *Morgan Evans,* of *Pentre.* The second at *Swansea,* the second Wednesday and Thursday in June; Brother *William Williams,* of *Ebenezer,* to

preach

preach, or Brother G. *Rees*. The third to be at Salem (*Roe*), the firſt Wedneſday and Thurſday in July, Brother *Zechariah Thomas* to preach, or Brother *Morris Jones*.

Some of the miniſters having adviſed Brother *Zechariah Thomas* to draw up a ſketch on church diſcipline, and propoſe it for a circular letter; he did ſo, and read it at the Aſſociation. After a very little amendment, it was agreed to by the whole body. This was a very prudent ſtep to aſſiſt the young churches, and to promote order, and ſome degree of uniformity through the whole, though now in three bodies, or diſtricts. A large impreſſion was ſoon ſubſcribed for.

This year died Mr. *Morgan Harris*, the acceptable aſſiſting colleague at *Llanwenarth*; his father and grandfather had been worthy paſtors at *Blaenau*. After the Aſſociation died Mr. *David Evans*, the truly valuable paſtor at *Dolau*, who was appointed to preach at the very next Aſſociation. He had exerted himſelf much to promote the infant cauſe in *North Wales*, and indeed planned the miſſion for that part of the Principality.

The former and preſent names of the BAPTIST CHURCHES in WALES; the years they were reſpectively formed or received into the connexion, and the page in the preceding ſheets where ſome account is given of moſt of them.

No.	Names.	Years.	Page.	No.	Names.	Years.	Page.
1	Olchon	1633	3	12	Cilfowyr	1704	30
2	Ilſton	1649	5	13	Pen-y-fai	1726	43
	& Hay, including			14	Pentre	1727	ib.
	Olchon, revived in	1650	6	15	Pen-y garn	1729	44
3	Llanharan §	ib.	ib.	16	Moleſton	1731	45
4	Carmarthen	ib.	7	17	Llanelli	1735	48
5	Abergavenny	1652	8	18	Aberduar	1742	52
6	Ruſhacre	1668	21	91	Llangloffan	1745	53
7	Llangwm	*	23	20	Betheſda	1747	54
8	Blaenau	} 1696	26	21	Glyn	1764	60
9	Glandwr			22	Ebenezer	1767	62
10	Troſgoed	1699	ib.	23	Dark-gate	1768	ib.
11	Radnor	†	28	24	Caerleon	1771	‡65

§ The miſtake of Llanafan which has been put for Llanharan is rectified in the beginning of the Appendix to this hiſtory.

* Of Llangwm and Llantriſaint in Monmouthſhire ſee p. 23, and Appendix.

† Radnor, then including what is now called Dolau and Pentre. This church was formed probably before 1649, but perhaps mixt, and not in the connexion before 1700. ſee p. 29.

‡ But joined the connexion in 1772. The following dates moſtly ſhew the year when the churches joined the aſſociation.

25 Uſk

No.	Names.	Years.	Page.	No.	Names.	Year.	Page.
25	Ufk	1772	65	37	Ramoth	1786	71
26	Salem	1773	ib.	38	Yftrad		
27	Trofnant	1777	67	39	Llanfachreth		
28	Graig			40	Newbridge	1787	ib.
29	Priory-ftreet	1778	ib.	41	Neuadd, now Builth		
30	St Nicholas			42	Engine		
31	Ebenezer, Anglefea	1779	68	43	Lland-y-faen	1788	72
32	Beaumaris			44	2d Church Swanfea		
33	Roe, now Salem	1785	70	45	Aberyftwyth		
34	Twyngwyn			46	Nottage	1789	73
35	Nevin	1786	71	47	Bryn Salem		
36	Horeb			48	Neath	1790	74

The number of churches here is 48, but the old church at Caermarthen was diffolved in the troublefome times (See page 23). From Llanharan they removed to Llantrifaint in Glamorganfhire; in the perfecutions they exifted at Kelligâr and Craig-yr-allt, but at Hengoed fince 1710 (See p. 34, and Appendix). Llangwm and Llantrifaint in Monmouth-fhire diffolved about 1742 (See p. 52). So in 1790, the number was 46, but the following names are changed, Ilfton is now called Swanfea; Abergavenny, Llanwenarth; Rufhacre, Rhydwilim; Glandwr, Pant-têg, Trofgoed, Maes-y-berllan; Radnor, now Dolau. While the churches worfhipped in dwelling houfes they were obliged to fhift from one place to another, and as times changed, the names often changed. Several of the churches now meet in two counties, as Aberduar, Pant-têg, Graig, Cilfowyr, Ebenezer, &c. Thefe five are on the eaft or fouth of the river Teivy which divides Cardiganfhire from thofe of Pembroke and Car-marthen; yet all thefe five churches have many members, and a number of meeting-houfes and preaching places, in Cardiganfhire, where there have been Baptifts, and not a few, ever fince the Commonwealth, though no church is named there now but Aberyftwyth lately formed. Glandwr was in Cardiganfhire.

A List of the BAPTIST ASSOCIATIONS in the PRINCI-PALITY of WALES, &c. and of the Minifters who preach-ed at thofe Meetings, as near as they could be collected, with a reference to the pages in this hiftory where moft of them are mentioned.

Year.	Month.	Place.	Page.
1650	9th month	Ilfton	6
1651	1ft	Carmarthen	7
1653	5th	Abergavenny	8
1654	1ft	Aberafon	10
1654	6th	Llantrifaint	11

1655

Year.	Month.	Place.	Page.
1655	1st	Hay	14
1656	5th	Brecknock	15
1689	September	London	21
1690	June	Ditto	ib.
1691	June	Ditto	24
1692	May	Ditto	ib.
1693	April	Briftol	ib.
1694	April	Ditto	25
1695	March	Ditto	ib.
1696	November	Ditto	ib.
1697		Ditto	26
1698	June	Taunton	ib.
1699	Whitfun-week	Ditto	ib.

The two laft of thefe affociations were at Taunton, Somerfet; where Mr. Thomas Whinnel was then paftor. He was one of thofe who figned the Confeffion of Faith in the General Affembly at London in 1689. Here we have 18 affociations in the laft century; feven of them were held in Wales. Four of the above met in London, and the reprefentatives of feveral churches in Wales with them. The other feven were properly the Weftern affociation, to which letters, or meffengers, from the Principality were fent; a practice which continued for above half this century. And Pen-y-garn, one of the Welfh churches, appears in the Weftern Affociation letter fo late as 1770.

In the prefent Century it will be needlefs to infert the month of each meeting, if the following remarks are remembered. From 1700 to 1707, the time of meeting was in May or June; from thence until 1755 in the Whitfun-week; and from 1755 to 1790 it hath feldom failed to be on the fecond Wednefday and Thurfday of June. The two days are commonly named; but for many years the Brethren have met Tuefday afternoon, and feparated Thurfday afternoon. I have no account of any fermon preached at the affociation in the laft century, either in Wales, London, or Briftol; but meffengers met chiefly to confult for the benefit of the churches. The firft information I have of a fermon at an affociation, in the Principality, is in the letter of 1703, which appoints one to be preached the following year. The letters make no mention of the perfon who preached at the meeting, they only fay who was appointed for next time, and thus it continued to 1734. Crofby * fays, that a fermon was preached at the Affociation in London in 1704. Probably it begun in London and Wales the fame year. Thefe hints premifed, I proceed to the lift.

* In his hiftory of the Baptifts, vol. iv. p. 4.

Year.	Place.	Page.	Persons appointed to preach the ensuing year.
1700	Llanwenarth	27	
1701	Ditto	ib.	
1702	Swansea	28	
1703	Llanwenarth	29	Rich. Williams to preach next year
1704	Swansea	ib.	Philip James.
1705	Llanwenarth	30	Abel Morgan.
1706	Swansea	31	Morgan Griffiths.
1707	Llanwenarth	32	Nathan Davis, or Caleb Evans.
1708	Rhydwilim	ib.	John Jenkins, or Samuel Jones.
1709	Trosgoed	33	I have not the letter of this year,
1710		34	Nor this, so know not the place.
1711	Hengoed, probably,	35	I could never find the letter of 1711,
1712	Llanwenarth	37	Nor of 1712.
1713	Rhydwilim	ib.	Nathan Davis to preach next year.
1714	Swansea	38	
1715	Blaenau	ib.	
1716	Llanwenarth	ib.	John Jenkins, or Nathan Davis.
1717	Blaenau	ib.	Morgan Griffiths, or John Harris.
1718	Llanelli	39	
1719	Rhydwilim	ib.	John Jenkins, or John Harris.
1720	Trosgoed	ib.	John Harris, or Enoch Francis.
1721	Coomb	40	Enoch Francis, or Wm. Meredith.
1722	Hengoed	ib.	David James, or Nathan Davis.
1723	Llanwenarth	41	Nathan Davis, or Samuel Jones.
1724	Blaenau	ib.	Samuel Jones, or Wm. Meredith.
1725	Llanelli	42	Caleb Evans, or William Phillips.
1726	Cilfowyr	ib.	Nathan Davis, or Morgan Griffiths.
1727	Swansea	43	Morgan Jones, or Enoch Francis.
1728	Rhydwilim	ib.	Enoch Francis, or John Phillips.
1729	Llangloffan	44	John Jenkins, or Caleb Evans.
1730	Hengoed	ib.	
1731	Llanwenarth	45	Griffith Jones, or John Jenkins.
1732	Blaenau	ib.	John Jenkins, or Myles Harrys.
1733	Pen-y-fai	46	Enoch Francis, or Roger David.

Thus far there was only one sermon preached at the association. From this year forward, two in general, and sometimes more; particularly of late years. And from henceforth, the letters commonly inform us who preached, and on what text.

| 1734 | Pen-y-garn | 47 | Enoch Francis, Matt. xxiv. 45. Bernard Foskett, 2 Tim. iv. 7. |
| 1735 | Llanelli | ib. | Roger David only, 1 Tim. iv .16. |

WELSH ASSOCIATION, &c.

Year.	Place.	Page.	Persons who preached.
1736	Rhydwilim	48	Miles Harrys, Rom. x. 15.
			Hugh Evans, Eph. iii. 8.
1737	Newcastle	ib.	Morgan Griffiths, Acts xxvi. 28.
1738	Hengoed	50	Thomas Matthias, Jer. iii. 15.
1739	Llanwenarth	ib.	Griffith Jones, 1 Cor. iv. 1, 2.
			Hugh Evans, Phil. iv. 8.
1740	Cilfowyr	ib.	Morgan Harris, Job xxxiii. 23.
			Hugh Evans, 2 Kings ii. 14.
1741	Blaenau	51	David Owen, 1 Cor. xvi. 10.
			Bernard Foskett, 1 Thess. i. 5.
1742	Llangloffan	52	Griffith Davis, and Hugh Evans
1743	Cilfowyr	ib.	Miles Harrys, Jer. xv. 19.
			Evan Jenkins, 2 Tim. ii. 19.
1744	Pen-y-garn	53	Dav. Thomas, Cilfowyr, 1 Chro. xxix. 1.
			Hugh Evans, Isa. lxii. 6, 7.
1745	Pentre	ib.	Thomas Edwards, 2 Tim. ii. 15.
			Evan Jenkins, Heb. xii. 15.
1746	Swansea	ib.	Griffith Jones, 2 Chron. xv. 7.
			Evan Jenkins, Jude 21.
1747	Brechfa	54	Evan Thomas, John xxi. 17.
			Evan Jenkins, 1 Thess. ii. 12.
1748	Garth	ib.	Griffith Jones, 1 Cor. ii. 2.
			Hugh Evans, 2 Cor. v. 20.
1749	Llanelli	ib.	Griffith Thomas, 2 Cor. v. 11.
			Dav. Thomas, Cilfowyr, Matt. xxii. 4.
			Griffith Jones, 2 Cor. xiii. 2.
1750	Moleston	55	Evan Jenkins, Matt. xvi. 18.
			John Thomas, 2 Tim. iv. 5.
1751	Hengoed	56	Griffith Davis and Evan Jenkins.
1752	Aberduar	ib.	Edmund Watkins, Mark xvi. 15.
			Caleb Harris, Col. iv. 3, 4.
1753	Maesdorglwyd	ib.	Dav. Thomas, Cilfowyr, 1 Tim. iv. 16.
			Griffith Davis, Eph. iii. 8.
1754	Rhydwilim	ib.	Caleb Harris, 2 Tim. ii. 25.
			Miles Harrys, 1 Cor. xv. 34.
1755	Bethesda	ib.	Rich. Jones, 2 Tim. iv. 2.
			Hugh Evans, 2 Tim. ii. 1.
1756	Llandyfyl	57	Miles Harrys, Rev. xiv. 6, 7.
			Griffith Davis, Acts v. 42.
1757	Llanwenarth	ib.	Timothy Thomas, 1 Cor. ix. 16.
			Hugh Evans.
1758	Llangloffan,	ib.	David Owen, Col. iv. 17.
			Hugh Evans, 1 Cor. i. 23, 24.

Year.	Place.	Page.	Persons who preached.
1759	Blaenau	58	Evan Thomas, Luke xii. 42.
			Hugh Evans, Acts xx. 24.
1760	Cilfowyr	ib.	Edmund Watkins, Luke xiv. 23.
			Benjamin Francis, Titus ii. 14.
1761	Pen-y-garn	59	Dav. Thomas, Newcastle, Mat. xxi. 42.
			Hugh Evans, Rom. i. 16.
1762	Peatre	ib.	John Williams, Col. i. 28.
			Benjamin Francis, 1 Pet. ii. 2.
1763	Swansea	60	Dav. Thomas, Rhydwilim. Psa. li. 13.
			Hugh Evans, Eph. iv. 12, 13.
			Caleb Evans, Phil. ii. 1.
1764	Maes-y-berllan	ib.	Lewis James, 2 Tim. ii. 15.
			Hugh Evans, Hof. xiv. 5.
1765	Dolau	ib.	George Rees, 1 Pet. v. 2.
			Benjamin Francis, Micah ii. 7.
1766	Llanelli	61	Timothy Thomas, Isa. xxvii. 13.
			Hugh Evans, Zech. xiv. 20.
1767	Molefton	62	Griffith Davis, Col. i. 28.
			Caleb Evans, Briftol, Col. iii. 11.
1768	Hengoed	ib.	Dav. Thomas, Newcaftle, 2 Cor. iv. 5.
			Samuel Stennett, Matt. xxviii. 20.
1769	Aberduar	63	Dav. Thomas, Rhydwilim, 2 Cor. v. 14.
			Benjamin Francis, Rev. iii. 19.
1770	Chapel-y-ffin	ib.	John Williams, Acts xxvi. 22, 23.
			Hugh Evans, Mal. ii. 15.
1771	Pen-y-fai	64	Wm. Williams, 2 Cor. v. 11.
			Benjamin Francis, Pfalm cxxvi. 6
1772	Rhydwilim	ib.	Griffith Davis, 2 Cor. v. 20.
			Wm. Williams, Heb. xii. 2.
1773	Bethefda	65	John Williams, Matt. xxii. 4.
			Hugh Evans, Zech. i. 5.
1774	Ebenezer	ib.	Edmund Watkins, Acts xx. 26, 27.
			Benjamin Francis, 1 Cor. xv. 58.
1775	Ufk	ib.	W. Williams, Hof. vii. 9.
			Hugh Evans, Heb. xii. 22, 23.
			Thomas Hiller, Luke viii. 35.
1776	Pant-têg	66	John Thomas, Deut. xxxiii. 3.
			Benjamin Francis, Phil. i. 27.
			Joshua Thomas, Pfalm xlii. 5. preceding evening.
1777	Caerleon	67	George Rees, 1 Cor. v. 18.
			Hugh Evans, Luke xii. 43.

1778

Year.	Place.	Page.	Persons who preached.
1778	Salem	67.	Thomas Phillips, Acts xv. 16.
			Benjamin Francis, Luke x. 2.
1779	Glyn	68.	John Williams, John i. 1—3.
			Samuel Medley, Zech. ix. 16, 17.
			Stephen Davis, Matt. xvi. 24.
			George Rees, xi. 21.
1780	Llanwenarth	ib.	Zecharias Thomas, Gal. vi. 14.
			Caleb Evans, of Bristol, 1 Tim. i. 15.
			Benjamin Francis, 1 Theff. ii. 13.
			David Evans, Eph. i. 23.
1781	Llangloffan	69.	Wm. Williams, Heb. iii. 7, 8.
			John Thomas, Jer. iii. 23.
			Benjamin Francis, Matt. xxv. 21.
1782	Blaenau	ib.	James Thomas, Tuesday evening.
			George Rees, Zech. iii. 4.
			Benjamin Francis, Zech. xiv. 3.
1783	Cilfowyr	ib.	Morgan Rees, 1 Pet. ii. 4.
			Miles Edwards, Pf. xciii. 5.
			Thomas Thomas, Rom. v. 11.
1784	Pen-y-garn	ib.	David Evans, of Graig, Zech. ix. 9.
			Caleb Evans, of Bristol, Pf. cxix. 128.
			John Richard, Luke ii. 10.
			Henry David, John i. 14.
			Benjamin Morgan, Zech. iv. 8.
1785	Graig	70.	Z. Thomas, Cant. ii. 9.
			David Jones, 1 Tim. i. 10.
			Thomas Thomas, John viii. 32.
1786	Pentre	ib.	Miles Edwards, Pfalm xxxvi. 7.
			Henry David, Jer. xv. 19.
			Caleb Evans, of Bristol, 1 John iv. 10.
			George Rees, 2 Cor. v. 4.
1787	Priory-street	71.	David Jones, Mal. i. 11.
			Thomas Thomas, 1 John ii. 3.
			Job David, 2 Cor. iv. 7.
			Timothy Thomas, Ifa. liii. 10
1788	Llannerchmedd	72.	Morgan Rees, Hab. iii. 9.
			D. Powell, Matt. xvii. 2 6.
			Gabriel Rees, Luke xxiv. 26.
			Benjamin Phillips, Exod. iii. 3.
			David Evans, Rev. i. 20.
			Benjamin Davis, John iii. 19.
			Henry David, Eph. iii. 8.
			David Evans, Pfalm cxlix. 2.
			Timothy Thomas, Ifa. xiv. 32.

Year.	Place.	Page.	Persons who preached.
1789	Maes-y-berllan	ib.	William Williams, Neh. viii. 2.
			Caleb Evans, of Bristol, Acts xv. 9.
			George Rees, 1 Tim. vi. 6.
			Benjamin Francis, Rom. vi. 15.
1790	Dolau	73.	Edmund Watkins, Luke xiv. 22, 23.
			Benjamin Francis, Phil. iii. 16.
			J. Evans, 2 Cor. iv. 7.
			David Jones, Isa. lx. 7.
			Joshua Thomas, Jos. xxi. 45.

EXPLANATORY HINTS.

The attentive Reader is referred to page 76, above, regarding the change of names of several places. Page 75, 76, give the dates when most of the churches were formed. But in the list of the Associations, Llanelli and Llangloffan appear before the dates when churches were incorporated in these places. There are also other instances where the annual meeting was kept in some capital branch of the church; hence it is, that there are names in the latter list, which appear not in that of the churches, such as these; Brechfa, the place of meeting in 1747, belonged to Maes-y-berllan, and was thought convenient; and before that, Coomb, where the Association met in 1721, is called Radnor in the list of churches. Garth, mentioned in 1748, was a place belonging to Dolau. Maesdorglwyd under 1753, and Chapel-y-ffin 1770, belonged to Olchon, and were convenient places for the Association. Newcastle, 1737; Llandysyl, 1756; and Pant-teg, 1776, constituted the very same church, only the meetings were kept in different places for conveniency; and perhaps there are some other instances of this sort.

The following worthy characters ought to be distinguished here. They were not properly of the Association; yet they voluntarily took long journies at their own expence, generally preached in English, and repeated a little in Welsh. The truly reverend Hugh Evans, M. A. mentioned above, p. 67, appears by the foregoing list, to have preached at the Association seventeen times. Mr. Evan Jenkins, of Wrexham, appears in the above list in 1743. It pleased God to remove him by death before the Association of 1752. Yet in that short space he stands in the list six times. He was very acceptable, and ripened apace for a better state. Our very worthy friend Rev. Caleb Evans, D. D. should not be omitted here, though he did not understand Welsh. He is upon the list as early as 1763; and preached in all six times. These three are gone to rest. But our great and warm friend Benjamin Francis, M. A. is yet on the stage. His name appears in 1760, and since then he has preached fourteen times in the course of thirty years. One of the fourteen happened to be omitted in the list, but it appears in page 67, under the year 1777.

AN INDEX OF THE NAMES IN THE PRECEDING HISTORY.

N. B. Those in small capitals were not Baptists: and a few known not to have been natives of Wales are in Italics.

A

Name	Page
Mr. Abbot	17, 19, 20

B

Name	Page
Isaac Backus	5, 17
John Boggs	49
William Bound	18
Evan Bowen	8, 18
Stephen Brace	10
Simon Butler	36

C

Name	Page
Thomas Carter	8
William Chaffey	ib.
Robert Cherry	ib.
William Combey	ib.
William Confet	ib.
WALTER CRADOCK	3, 4, 86
JOHN CRAGG	10, 17
Dr. CRISP	44

D

Name	Page
David Davis	6, 7, &c. 19
David Davis, America	34, 35
Leyson Davis	9
John Davis	14
Hugh Davis, America	36, 37
John Davis, his Affiftant	37
James Davis, America	36
John Davis, Swanfea	43, 52
Nathan Davis	29, 32, 43
JAMES DAVIS, of Merthyr	46
William Davis, America	40, 49
Griffith Davis	51, 66
Thomas Davis	54, 70
Thomas Davis, Rock	57
David Davis, Aberduar	63
Benjamin Davis	72
Samfon Davis	ib.
Stephen Davis	68
Evan David	25
Evan David, Bethefda	54, 72
John David	25
Thomas David	51, 62
Roger David	43, 52
Morgan David	51
Thomas David, Cilfowyr	70
Mofes David	62
Jenkin David	71
Job David	ib.
Henry David	72
Rees David	ib.
James Drewett	64
Charles Doe	46
John Duckfield	61

E

Name	Page
Joseph Eaton	35, 49
Isaac Eaton, his Son	24
Thomas Edwards	10
Morgan Edwards, M. A.	52, 59
Nicholas Edwards	39
Evan Edwards	42, 64
Watkin Edwards, his Son	64
Thomas Edwards	53, 54
Miles Edwards his Son	67, 69
John Edwards	17, 18, 20, 22
James Edwards	64
William Erbury	3, 4
Thomas Evans	
Caleb Evans	
John Evans	
Hugh Evans, M. A.	8
Caleb Evans, D. D.	
John Evans	
Hugh Evans, Radnorfhire	18
John Evans	28, 31
John Evans, America	35
David Evans, Cilfowyr	55
David Evans, Conwil	62
David Evans, Dolau	67, 75
David Evans, Bigglefwade	71
David Evans, Thorn	72
David Evans, Graig	70
Rees Evans	54, 63
Peter Evans	64
Caleb Evans	65
Morgan Evans	66, 74
BENJAMIN EVANS	73

F

Name	Page
Bernard Foskett	47, 51
GEORGE FOX	17
Enoch Francis	37, 51
Abel Francis	42, 46
Jonathan Francis	52
Benjamin Francis	59, 68, 72

G

Name	Page
Daniel Garnon	67
Charles Garfon	10, 15
Samuel George	62
Francis Giles	18, 20
John Gill, D. D.	55, 56
Edward Green	10
Henry Gregory	18, 20, 27
Griffith Griffiths	11
Harry Griffiths	14
Thomas Griffiths	25, 28
Morgan Griffiths	25, 27, 50
John Griffiths	29
Evan Griffiths, Efq.	31
Benjamin Griffiths, America	34, 41
Abel Griffiths, his Son	35
Samuel Griffiths	61
John Griffiths, his Father	

F 2   Jon.

INDEX OF NAMES.

H.
	Page.
John Harris	37, 43, 49.
Morgan Harris, his Son	47, 51, 54.
Morgan Harris, his Son	75.
Miles Harris	42, 44, 45, 66.
Caleb Harris	54, 56.
Charles Harris	66.
William Harris	70.
Richard Harrison	16.
Anthony Harry	10, 15, 17.
Thomas Henry	62.
William Herbert	48, 52.
Thomas Hiller	65.
Robert Hopkins	10.
John Hopkins	68.
Griffith Howell	21, 25, 31.
James Hugh	11.
Samuel Hugh	36.
William Hughes	69.
David Hughes	71.

I.
Jacob Isaac	56.

J.
Thomas James	10, 15.
David James	22.
James James	24, 47.
Joshua James	29, 44.
Philip James	30, 33.
Samuel James, his Son	30.
John James, America	35.
John James, Rhydwilim	53, 60.
David James	38, 42.
Lewis James	60, 64.
Nathaniel Jenkins, America	33, 35.
John Jenkins	25, 40——47.
Evan Jenkins, his Son	52——56.
Joseph Jenkins, D. D. his Son	52.
EVAN JOHN	46.
Thomas Jones	10, 15, 17.
Thomas Jones, America	44, 48, 49.
Samuel Jones, D. D.	49.
Morgan Jones	14, 17, 18.
Morgan Jones	ib.
Morgan Jones, Swansea	29, 36, 45.
Morgan Jones, L.L.D. his Grandson	55.
Richard Jones	15.
Richard Jones, Dolau	56, 63.
Jenkin Jones	16, 17, 19.
Jenkin Jones, America	34.
William Jones	20, 21, 25, 27, 31.
Robert Jones	22.
Samuel Jones, America	24, 28, 35.
Sam. Jones, Cilsowyr	25, 30, 42, 48.
SAM. JONES, Glamorganshire	25.
Griffith Jones	42, 43, 50——55.
George Jones	24, 25.
Philip Jones	39, 40.
Philip Jones, Upton	40.
Edmund Jones, his Son	40.
EDMUND JONES Monmouthshire	45, 48.
Rees Jones	51, 53, 62.
Rees Jones, Pentre	66, 72.
Isaac Jones, his Son	66.
David Jones, Wrexham	68.
David Jones, Llanwenarth	64.
David Jones, Pen-y-garn	68.
Morris Jones	75.
Thomas Joseph	9, 15, 19.

K.
Benjamin Keach	25, 48.

L.
Thomas Lewis	10.
Thomas Lewis, Exeter	65.
Timothy Lewis	37, 40.
JENKIN LEWIS	46.
David Lewis, Hengoed	50.
David Lewis, Llangloffan	55.
Francis Lewis	69.
Thomas Llewelyn, L.L.D.	52, 66, 69.
James Lodwick	54, 60.

M.
Isaac Marlow	23.
Hugh Matthews	12, 14.
Anthony Matthews	36.
Simon Matthews	ib.
William Matthews	ib.
Thomas Matthias	37, 47, 53.
Samuel Medley	68.
Arthur Melchior	36.
William Meredith	40, 52.
John Mildmay	8.
William Milman	17, 20, 22.
JOHN MOON	17, 18.
Robert Morgan	10, 15, 17, 20, 33.
Nathaniel Morgan	22, 41, 43.
Abel Morgan	26, 35, 37, 38, 41.
Enoch Morgan, his Brother	32, 34.
Abel Morgan	32.
John Morgan	33.
Robert Morgan of London	33, 34.
Philip Morgan	41, 46, 48, 66.
John Morgan, Cilfowyr	51, 59.
John Morgan, Maes-y-berllan	72.
Henry Morgan	54.
William Morgan	ib.
David Morris	71.
Seth Morris	ib.
Thomas Morris	72.
John Myles	5, 9, 10, 14, 17, 18, 21.
Richard Myles	36.

N.
John Norent	25.
John D. Nicholas	51, 60.

O.
JAMES OWEN	25.
David Owen	44, 48, 61.
David Owen, his Son	69.

Thomas

INDEX OF NAMES.

P.
	Page.
Thomas Parry	10, 20, 33, 34.
John Penry	5.
——— Perrott	45.
William Phillips	29, 38, 49.
William Phillips, Bethesda	51.
John Phillips	41, 44.
Henry Phillips	64.
Thomas Phillips	67, 68.
Benjamin Phillips	72.
John Piggot	34.
Vavafor Powell	4, 16, 18, 20, 86.
David Powell	72.
John Price	18.
John Price, Llanwenarth	68.
Joseph Price	40,
Thomas Price	29, 40.
Christopher Price	18, 20, 21—26.
Wm. Prichard	9, 10, 15, 21, 29, 31.
Walter Proffer	6, 15, 16, 17, 19.
Thomas Proud	9, 17, 19.

Q.
Thomas Quarrel	20, 22, 33, 43.

R.
Thomas David Rees	25, &c. 31, 32.
David Rees	34, 45, 46, 47.
Peter Rees	33.
Jacob Rees	50.
George Rees	60, 63, 68.
Morgan Rees, Llanelli	69.
Morgan Rees, Pen-y-garn	72.
Gabriel Rees	ib.
David Richard	50, 53, 55.
William Richards	73.
John Richard	51, 62, 63.
Daniel Rogers	46.
Richard Roffer	10, 15.
William Rider	48.

S.
Joseph Stafford	8.
Joseph Stennett, D. D.	34.
Samuel Stennett, D. D.	22, 41, 62.
John Spencer	22.
——— Sorency	36.
Evan Saundars	52.
David Saundars	63.

T.
William Thomas	9, 15, 17, 19.
Howell Thomas	ib.
Lewis Thomas	29, &c. 27, 30.
Rhydderch Thomas	15.
John Thomas	25.
Owen Thomas, America	32.
Elisha Thomas, America	ib.

	Page.
Morgan Thomas	36.
William Thomas, America	37.
John Thomas	ib.
Timothy Thomas, Pershore	39.
Tim. Thomas, Aberduar	52, 69, &c.
Timothy Thomas, Graig	70.
Evan Thomas	47, 48, 69.
Evan Thomas, Bridgwater	57.
David Thomas, Cilfowyr	50, 54, 65.
David Thomas, Pant-têg	59, 62, 69.
David Thomas, Rhydwilim	60.
John Thomas	52, 58, 61, 71.
Griffith Thomas	53, 54, 60.
Joshua Thomas, Leominster	54, 55, 56.
Joshua Thomas, Lymington	63.
William Thomas, Blaenau	58.
Zechariah Thomas	63, 68, 75.
Thomas Thomas	63, 69.
Daniel Thomas, Henley	63.
Daniel Thomas, Rhydwilim	69.
James Thomas	69, 72.
Lewis Thomas	73.
John Tombs, B. D.	10.
Samuel Tull	8.

V.
Howell Vaughan	3, 10.
Henry Vaughan	10.

W.
Roger Walker	41, 50, 54, 57.
Fowler Walker	46, 47.
Thomas Watkins	10, 15, 17, 20, &c.
Howell Watkins	10.
Edmund Watkins	52, 56, 73.
William Watkins	63.
Richard Watkins	69.
Henry Williams	18, 20.
Walter Williams	22.
William Williams, Olchon	46, 64.
Wm. Williams, Ebenezer	62, 64, 74.
Wm. Williams, Maes-y-berllan	71.
Morgan Williams	22.
Rich. Williams	25, 27, &c. 40, &c.
David Williams	46.
James Williams	37, 39, 50, 53.
Daniel Williams, D. D.	44.
Thomas Williams	47, 52.
Griffith Williams	47.
John Williams	59, 64, 68.
Samuel Wilson	57.
Charles Winter	44, 47, 51, 55.
——— Woolaston	23.
——— Wroth	3, 4.

Among these names there are a few who were not Ministers; but they were either eminently useful to the churches at home, or as emigrants to America *. It is not now certain how many of the messengers

* America, or Am. after a name, denotes that the person emigrated to that country.

of the churches in the time of the Commonwealth were preachers; but, as they attended the Affociations, feveral of them are recorded here.

This Index contains perhaps the names of all the minifters mentioned in the preceding Tract; but they are not referred to here as often as fome of them are named, yet, in general, their firft appearance in the Affociation, and their clofe of life, is referred to.

This is not pretended to be a hiftory of the Welfh churches, but of the Affociations, and of the Minifters *chiefly* concerned in them; a number prayed at thofe meetings who are not named here; and there are minifters of the laft century mentioned here who were not in the Affociation.

GENERAL OBSERVATIONS.

1. Though moft of the Baptifts in the Principality have been in connexion with the Affociation from the beginning of this century, however it was before, yet there have been fome of them in that country ever fince 1640, or earlier, who never entered into this connexion. The 4th and 5th pages of this Hiftory inform us how active Meff. Cradock and Powell were, who encouraged mixed communion of Pædo and Antipædo Baptifts. Probably every congregation of Nonconformifts in that country, except Olchon, were of mixed principles, till Mr. J. Myles and his friends formed a church of profeffed Baptifts, in 1649. Mr. Cradock refided fome time at Wrexham; and Mr. Vavafor Powell near Newtown, in Montgomeryfhire: their congregations were profeffedly mixed. Some years after the death of Mr. Morgan Lloyd, at Wrexham, Mr. John Evans (father of the late Dr. John Evans, author of Sermons on the Chriftian Temper), fettled there about 1668. The people were mixed; he and they were friendly. When any one wifhed to be baptized, Mr. Thomas Loe, of Warrington, moftly adminiftered the ordinance to them. Mr. Evans died about 1700. He was fucceeded by Mr. Jenkin Thomas; and he by Mr. John Williams, both Independents: but the latter, upon conviction, was baptized by immerfion about 1715. The minifters have been Baptifts ever fince; and the church remained mixed till lately, if it is not fo now. For many years the Independents in communion were very few. This people never were in the Affociation. Mr. V. Powell's church was moftly in Montgomeryfhire; it lay very wide, and was mixt. He was fucceeded by Mr. Henry Williams, and the latter by Mr. Reynold Wilfon: thefe were Baptifts; but they had alfo Independent colleagues. —The Society was divided into three; but there has been no Baptift-minifter refident with either of them fince about 1737. Llanbrynmair is now by far the chief congregation of the three, in which there are but few Baptifts at prefent. But this church of Mr. Vavafor Powell's was never in the Affociation.

There was formerly a fmall Baptift congregation at Glafcoomb, Radnorfhire; but it does not appear that they ever had more than one paftor, Mr. Thomas Lewis, who died in 1735, and the few members did not long furvive. They did not belong to the Affociation,

2. About

GENERAL OBSERVATIONS.

2. About 1740, quarterly meetings were fet up: thefe were a kind of inferior Affociations: two minifters preached, and feveral prayed; the afternoon generally was fpent in improving converfation and confultation for the welfare of the churches. Thofe meetings are now numerous, divided into convenient diftricts.

3. When ftrangers hear that at an Affociation nine or ten thoufand people attend, more or lefs as the place is more or lefs central, they may well wonder how all can be accommodated. The manner of doing it is briefly thus: a piece of ground is taken, near to the meeting-houfe, which is kept up early in the Spring, and by June the grafs is good. Before 1790, when the Affociation was divided into three, it was fometimes neceffary to prepare for feven or eight hundred horfes, which graze in the time of fervice: two or three perfons were appointed to take care of them. The inhabitants, for five or fix miles round the place, provide lodgings for the ftrangers, and good entertainment for man and horfe, gratis. The generofity of the country is fuch, that, at thefe times, all defcriptions of perfons open their doors cordially, whether religious or not, gentlemen as well as farmers. The leading men of the congregation know before hand where to fend two, four, fix, or more guefts, and there are perfons prefent ready to take them to their refpective lodgings. On the Tuefday evening there is a meeting, almoft on purpofe to accommodate the ftrangers. They generally take their horfes with them; and where they lodge that night they are commonly the next. The chief public day is the Wednefday. Thurfday in the afternoon they fet out on their return. They fup and breakfaft where they lodge. The people before-hand bake a quantity of good bread, and brew good table-beer, and put it in the veftry, or fome convenient place; this, with cheefe and butter, makes their dinner on Wednefday, which they take, in and about the meeting-houfe on tables, boards, and as they can. As no meeting-houfe will contain the people, a temporary pulpit is prepared in the moft convenient place, that the auditory may hear in the houfe and out: it is fo covered as to prevent the fun and rain from coming to the minifter. The multitude is peculiarly numerous on the Wednefday, as all the neighbourhood flock together on that day. The accommodations are made at the expence of the church where the Affociation meets, but travelling expences lie upon the meffengers and the churches which fend them.

4. Of late years, the exclufions in thefe churches make a difagreeable appearance, and it will be well to be very cautious in admitting members; but when crowds make a profeffion, which has been happily the cafe of late years, it is no wonder there fhould be ftony-ground hearers among them. And in judging of this cafe, we are to confider the number of members in a church. There the number of the whole is fmall, it would be a wide breach to exclude ten or more in a year; but when the members of a church are from fix to eight hundred or more, the cafe is materially altered. It is a good evidence of the care in difcipline, when there are righteous

righteous exclusions. If persons come in unawares, when discovered they are cast out. The number of their restored annually is very considerable, which is an additional proof of their care and discipline.

5. Mr. Morgan Edwards's "Materials towards a History of the Baptists in Pennsylvania" mention and describe ten *first-day* Baptist churches in that province in 1770. The major part of the constituents and ministers of these were from the ancient Britons.

1. *Penne-peck*, now *Lower Dublin*, the first Baptist church in the province, formed in Jan. 1687-8; consisted then of eleven members, and their then pastor, for a short time. Of the eleven, five were from Wales; one of whom, Mr. Samuel Jones, was the most useful member in that church for thirty-four years; a considerable part of that time he preached to them as assistant, pastor, or colleague, See above page 24. The chief pastors of that church since have been Messr. Evan Morgan, Samuel Jones, Abel Morgan, Jenkin Jones; and the present Dr. Samuel Jones, all natives of the Principality. This church has had Englishmen for pastors, or ministers, about thirty years of the time since 1688.

2. The next Baptist church there was at *Welsh Tract*. The constituents and first pastor were from Wales; and all the pastors from 1701 to 1769, were from the same country. See page 28, 32, 34, 35.

3. The third church there was at *Great Valley*, formed in 1711. They likewise, pastor and church, were from Wales. And so was their second pastor. These two served the church honourably from 1711 to 1778. See page 35, 36, 37.

4. The next church in the Materials is *Brandiwine*. Though the constituents there seem to have been a mixture of English and Welsh, and first and second pastor natives of America, yet they were formed by Mr. Abel Morgan's help; and the second pastor was son of a minister from Wales.

5. *Montgomery*, constituted 1719; the members chiefly from Wales, and their ministers from the same country. See page 34, 35, 37, 41, and also Mr. Edwards's Materials.

6. *Tulpehokon*. Of the pastor and constituents, see page 48, 49.

7. *Southampton*, according to Mr. Edwards's Materials, is a kind of mixture of English and Welsh.

8. *Philadelphia* is said to have been formed, or re-constituted, in 1746; he first and second pastor from Wales. Of Mr. Jenkin Jones, see a hint page 34, of Mr. M. Edwards, page 52, 59.

9. *New Britain*, to be sure, from Wales; the ministers, and most of the constituents, to 1770, (see page 49.

10. *Konolowa*, the youngest church in the province in 1770, was formed in 1765. The constituents, by their names, seem not to have originated from Wales; but their first pastor did, though probably he himself was born in America.

This sketch shews that Wales is to be considered as the parent of the Baptist denomination in Pennsylvania.

THE END.

www.ingramcontent.com/pod-product-compliance
Lightning Source LLC
Chambersburg PA
CBHW032242080426
42735CB00008B/963